Man Up
MAN'S SEARCH FOR MEANING

RSI
PUBLISHING

DENNIS L TAYLOR

Scriptures are taken from the New International Version of the Bible
Books may be ordered through booksellers or by contacting:
Dennis Taylor
luke252.dennis@gmail.com

Raising the Standard International Publishing L. L. C.
https://www.rsipublishing.com
Navarre, Florida

ISBN: 9781960641274
Printed in the United States of America
Edition Date: November 2023

TABLE OF CONTENTS

DEDICATION

I wanted to dedicate this book to my dad, Donald Kenneth Taylor. Not because he was my earthly father but because of the man he was. He showed me love, and he taught me about what is right and wrong. He was a man of integrity and cared about the people around him. He taught me how to look someone in the eyes, give them my attention, and shake their hand firmly. He showed me how to work hard, provide for my family, and treat others fairly. He lived out in front of me how I was to love my wife and honor her. He punished me when I got out of hand. Yes, it put the fear of the Lord in me. He told me about Jesus and led me to Christ. Then, he poured everything into me and covered me with prayers and grace. I sure do miss him. But I will see him again one day!

My father is and always will be my hero. Growing up, he was always a constant in my life. He never missed a game and rarely ever missed a practice. He was a great dad to me and always took up time with my buddies who didn't have a dad. Growing up, we had a set of concrete weights with a metal bar. My brother and I would mess around with them in the yard. I remember loading up the bar with 110 lbs. and trying to deadlift it. We were getting it done. It was all I could do to pull that weight to my waist. Then my dad showed up and said, "I can pick that up with one hand over my head." There was no way. He bent over and grabbed that long bar with 110 lbs. of concrete weight. Then he loudly grunted and threw that weight over his head. At that point in my life, I pictured him as Superman. You see, my dad had guns. (Big biceps) As a child, I feared nothing when I was with my dad. I knew he was watching over me, and I knew he would protect me no matter what. I was in the presence of a superhero.

Dad, this book is all about what you taught me. I pray that you are pleased. I honor you today. To God be the glory!

INTRODUCTION

I am living in what I call the last one-third of my life. That thought is remarkably sober, but I am speaking the truth. No one wants to talk about their death, but it is a reality, and sooner or later, we all will take our last breath on this Earth. I don't know about you, but I want my life to count for something besides self-serving ambitions and selfish dreams. With that thought in mind, as I spent some time alone with God, I began to ask myself some direct questions. Questions like this: What made the most significant impact on my life? How did the positive change happen to me to become a godly husband and dad? The Lord knows I am imperfect, but my time alone with Him has set me up for success. My time alone with my Heavenly Father has directed me down that narrow path to Heaven. He has placed my feet on solid ground and has blessed me with godly wisdom. Did all of this just happen? No, but God gave us a plan in His Word to rise up and overcome. He has given us everything we need as men to live a life that pleases Him.

As I sat in the presence of the Lord, He began to pour out His Word and gave me direction as to what I needed to share. Then, I started writing His words to me in my War Journal. I patiently waited as He began to reveal a step-by-step process that has taken place in my life that has led me to a vibrant relationship with Him. God has shown me so many things over the years, even though I resisted and refused to surrender to His will fully. Then my mind began to wander, and I asked myself another question: If I could

1

speak to thousands and thousands of men, what would I share with them that can turn their lives around and set their course on a road that makes God smile?

Some people have told me that it's crazy to spend so much time writing a book for men. I understand what they are saying. It is proven that most men do not buy and read books. I get it, but I don't write to sell books. I write because God has called me to encourage and push others close to Christ. If one man reads this book, changes his life, and is pulled into a life that inspires others, it will be worth it.

Rise up, O men of God! It is time to "Man Up" and become the spiritual leaders of your family. Man up and become that godly husband and dad that He has called us to be. It is time to dive into a deeper walk with our Heavenly Father and seek His face. It is time to soak in His presence, study His Word, and spend quality time talking and listening to God. When did you last stop long enough to take a spiritual check-up? Where do you fall when it comes to your spiritual growth? Do you have someone who holds you accountable? Are you following God's plan to share the love of Christ with a dark and dying world? Are we living out a lifestyle that is surrounded by discipleship? Are you living a life that the Holy Spirit dominates? Are we walking in Spirit and Truth?

So many questions, but how will you answer them? There is nothing in this book that you haven't heard before. No great secret will be revealed to you, but it will bring you back to the basics of the Christian faith. Men, we need to get back to the basics of Jesus' teaching and words, then live it out. Yes, put it into practice and be the man God has called us to be.

What are you waiting on? Dive in and get ready to live a life fully surrendered to the Savior of the world. I challenge you to make your time alone with God your highest priority in life. I dare you to pray and ask God to restore the joy of your salvation and give you an unquenchable desire to know Him most intimately. Rise up, O men of God!

Dennis L Taylor

Notes

CHAPTER ONE
A PSALMS ONE MAN

In this first chapter of Psalm, we will look at two men who lived two lives that ended up in two different destinies. Which of these two men do you connect with, or which one most resembles your life? We all have to make choices in this life, and every choice we make has a consequence with what we choose. Do you know what I am talking about? We all have made some bad choices, and we wish we could go back and change several things in our lives. Those bad choices lead to heartache, pain, and regret. Have you ever asked yourself, "What was I thinking?"

As I type this first chapter out, past regrets are popping up in my mind, one after another. What about you? Are there decisions you made in your past haunting you to this day? Is there a choice you made in relationships or your career that causes you nightmares and regrets? We all could probably fill up a book with story after story that makes us scratch our heads to this day. Have you ever made a wrong financial decision? It may have been a crazy, random purchase on the spur of the moment or when you robbed your 401K. Is it hitting home yet?

Listen, everyone is guilty of making poor decisions along the way, so don't feel like you are all alone. Hopefully, we have learned from our mistakes. Save your money now as a side note to those young dads with girls! Get ready because that wedding is just around the corner. You are thinking about how expensive those diapers are; think again. Set aside five dollars a paycheck, and don't touch it for any reason. If you get hungry, someone will feed you, but don't touch that money. You will need it later on. Let's read Psalm 1:1-3:

> *"Blessed is the man who does not walk in the counsel of the wicked or stand in the way of sinners or sit in the seat of mockers. But his delight is in the law of the Lord, and on his law, he meditates day and night. He is like a tree planted by streams of water, which yields its fruit in season and whose leaf does not wither. Whatever he does prospers."*

For those men who belong to Jesus Christ, the pattern and standard for our lives must never be determined by a fallen world or this earthly culture. When we want to know what kind of men we should be, we don't need to turn on the TV but open our Bibles. In God's Word, we find His will for our lives as men. I want to ask you three questions to get us thinking about what God calls us to be as men. The first question is this:

1. What is excluded from a Godly man's life?

These first few verses show what a prosperous man does not do. We know what he excludes from his life.

- **The advice and wisdom of this world are excluded.**

A Psalm's One man will not walk through life following the counsel of the ungodly-those who does not seek the Lord and His presence. He doesn't worry about what today's society is saying or proclaiming. His walk of life isn't dictated by what the world says is popular. The thinking of this world is selfish and humanistic. A Psalm One man does not live by the advice of earthly wisdom and philosophies. The second thing that he excludes from his life:

- **The ways of sinful man are excluded.**

He does not live the same way as men who practice sin and fall into temptation repeatedly with no remorse. I am talking about men who practice evil and celebrate it. It isn't that he has no association with them, but a Psalm One man finds himself in different environments that strengthen his relationship with the Lord. Men of God are called to be the light of the world; we are to reflect the glory of the Lord to the people around us. By coloring our lives with the same darkness as those who willingly live in sin, we will never be the world's light. The third thing the Psalm One Man excludes from his life is:

- **The attitude of scorners is excluded.**

A scorner is a person who mocks and scoffs at God and the things of God. A scoffer thinks nothing is sacred, and they have no fear of judgment or consequences for their wicked actions. The scoffer thinks Jesus is some lame storyteller who has nothing to do with how you live and carry on in everyday life. He cringes when God's name is mentioned. But a Godly man cringes when the Savior's name is belittled, or His name is used in vain.

Now, let's jump into the second question we need to ask ourselves as we dig into Psalm 1:

2. What produces this Godly man's joy?

It is incredible how many hours the average American spends on cell phones. I dare you to look at your cellphone and see how much screen time you spend each day on your device. How many hours a day do we look at other people's lives and get caught up in the web of deceit and sin? We have become fans of foolishness, which leaves us empty and searching. The Psalm One Man gets excited about the things of God. Look at what grabs his attention and helps him to live an authentic life of joy and happiness.

- **A Godly man's passion is for the Word of God.**

He hungers for God's Word and can't get enough of God's direction and wisdom. He receives pleasure when he opens up God's love note to us. He gets excited when others want to talk about the Bible and discuss the things of God. What are we genuinely enthusiastic about in this life? What gets us going in the morning? What is our passion? Is it college football? Is it the latest and greatest game called pickleball? When did you last sit down with friends and talk about the Bible instead of last night's playoff game? Not only was this man passionate about the Word, but he also noticed:

- **A Godly man applies the Word of God to his life.**

This man keeps talking over and thinking about the Word of God. In other words, he meditated on the Word of God. He held the Word of God in his mind and looked at how to apply it to daily life. God's instruction was at the forefront of his thought and not an afterthought. He became a student of the Word and learned how to hold it close to his heart. The Word of God was his go-to, and he leaned in the direction of God's instruction. Take notice not only his passion for the Word and his practice with the Word, but you have to see:

- **A Godly man sees The Word of God as his daily guide.**

He takes the text and carries it along with him throughout the day. Our time with God shouldn't be something we read at the beginning of our day, but it should be our daily guide. I challenge you today to hide God's Word in your heart. Plaster Scripture in your car and on the mirrors of your bathroom. Do you get excited when you open God's Word and hear from the very Creator of the world? Don't just read God's Word for knowledge; apply it to your life. After you read the Scripture, make sure you ask yourself five questions:

- **First question: Is there a sin I need to confess?**
- **Second question: Is there a promise I need to claim?**
- **Third question: Is there an attitude I need to change?**
- **Fourth question: Is there a command to obey?**
- **Fifth question: Is there an example to follow?**

3. *What makes this Godly man different?*

There is something about Psalm One Man that is different. Maybe he used to be just like everyone else; he was just a good ole boy who hung with the crowd and blended in. But in Christ, his heart and life were changed. What made him different? It was his:

- **He is rock-solid in Christ.**

Verse three says, "he shall be like a tree planted by streams of water." Not dropped or casually thrown out, but planted at a certain and for a specific reason. His life had stability because God placed him where he is, and he is securely planted in the will of God. So many men I know are not established in the Word of God; they never get settled and seem to be on an endless journey for peace and purpose in this life. They never get still and calm, so they never take root. Yes, the Psalm One Man is different, not only because of his stability in Christ but also for:

- **His strength comes from the Lord.**

Not only is he perfectly planted, but he is planted in a place he will never go without. He was rooted by streams of water. Not by one stream but by multiple streams. How good is God? If one stream dries up, he has already made provisions to care for our every need. Our God is never surprised or caught off guard. He is our provider and ensures we have everything we need. He satisfies our every longing.

What makes Psalm One Man so different? It's not only stability and his strength but also:

- **His success in life.**

Psalm 1:3: "He is like a tree planted by streams of water, which yields its fruit in season and whose leaf does not wither. Whatever he does prospers."

The Psalm One Man succeeds in the things of God. He will have spiritual fertility. In other words, the Godly Psalms One Man will grow and mature in the Lord and bring forth much fruit. He will be a healthy spiritual man who touches the lives of people around him. His walk with the Lord will not be marked with failure, losses, and struggles. There is nothing average about a Psalm One Man. He is daily dying to himself and seeking the face of God continually.

Every man wants to be blessed and happy. I think we all could agree on that. But there are very few who desire to be a godly man. Listen, only those willing to be the man described in Psalm One will ever know the kind of life described in this Scripture. This guy was your everyday kind of man, just like you and me. But by God's grace, we can venture through the Word of God and experience an exceptional and extraordinary life!

But it all begins and ends with Jesus Christ. Do you know Jesus as your Lord and Savior? Have you ever confessed your sins to the One who loves you the most? Have you ever died to "self" and surrendered your life to the King of Kings? Please read chapter two, and let me introduce you to my Savior and Lord. If we are going to build a house, we have to start with a good foundation. It's time to build our lives on a personal relationship with Jesus Christ.

Notes

CHAPTER TWO
DO YOU KNOW JESUS?

W e all have those times when we must tear down the walls we have allowed to exist. We all fall short, and we all mess up, and we do mess up along the way. But having a God who understands and shows us so much grace is good. "Thank you, Lord, for the gift of forgiveness and mercy. Thank you for lifting me and encouraging me daily. Thank you, God, for the privilege to come before you when I need to say, 'I am sorry.' Thank you for tearing down that old wall of sin in my heart." Yes, be thankful, but this is just the beginning of what God has for us as children of God. Not only does God want to break down the old walls of our lives, but He wants us to build a solid foundation. A foundation that is solid and will stand firm even when the worst storms come our way.

> *Matthew 7:24-25 Jesus tells us, "Therefore everyone who hears these words of mine and puts them into practice is like a wise man who built his house on the rock. The rain came down, the streams rose, and the winds blew and beat against that house; yet it did not fall, because it had its foundation on the rock."*

What is your life built on?

Before I go any further, I want to ensure you have a personal walk with Jesus Christ. Has there been a time in your life when you have come face to face with Jesus? Have you had an encounter with the Living God of the universe?

Being a Christian and a Christ follower isn't about our Church attendance. It is not about doing good deeds or being morally good. It's about a personal relationship with Jesus, making Him the foundation for everything, and knowing that the eternal God made a way for us to come to Him. Knowing and believing that He gave us His one and only Son to die on an old rugged cross, but also believing Jesus didn't stay in that grave. This foundation is alive and well today, knowing that Jesus overcame sin and death. "Thank you, Lord!"

Every builder needs to have a solid foundation. It needs to meet certain specifications. It has to be able to handle the weight of the load. That foundation in a believer's life is a personal relationship with Jesus Christ. When the storms come, and the water rises, will your foundation be able to stand? Money, power, position, and popularity will crumble under the weight of the load. Build on something that will last and stand the test of time. When we come to the end of ourselves and receive Jesus as our Lord and Savior, he becomes that foundation forever and ever. Yes, there will be tough times in life, and there will be struggles along the way.

> *Hebrews 13:5 reads, "Keep your lives free from the love of money and be content with what you have because God has said, "Never will I leave you; never will I forsake you."*

That is a promise from God Himself. He is my protector and my Heavenly Father. The great I AM—the God of Heaven and Earth. The all-knowing and all-powerful God of the universe, and I call Him Father because of what Jesus has done for me.

Oprah Winfrey has gone on record to say, "There are many ways to God." I want to go on record to say, "That is a lie from the very pits of Hell."

Jesus tells us in John 14:6, "I am the way, the truth, and the life. No one comes to the Father except through me."

In other words, Jesus said there is only one way to have a life-changing relationship with God. You can't be good enough to earn salvation or get a golden ticket to Heaven. You can go to Church every single time the door opens and still spend eternity in Hell forever and ever. You can study your Bible from cover to cover and memorize hundreds of Bible verses and still fall short of the Kingdom of God. You can be dunked in the baptismal pool at your Church so many times you become waterlogged and still be lost in Satan's web of lies. We serve a Holy God that can have nothing to do with sin. Sin separates us from God, and a price has to be paid for our sins. God had a plan, and He sent His only Son as a baby to be born of a virgin. This baby would live without sin and become God's perfect Lamb. He willingly laid down His life on that old, rugged cross for us.

Second Corinthians 5:21 says, "God made him "Jesus" who had no sin to be sin for us so that in him we might become the righteousness of God."

Jesus suffered, bled, and died for us. In other words, he took my place! He took my punishment and suffering. But the good news is this: death could not hold him; the grave could not keep him. Three days later, he arose from the grave, and he is alive and well today and sits at the

Father's right hand. But the most crucial point is that he rules upon the throne of my heart and has changed my life forever. "Thank you, Lord." That is the good news of Jesus in a nutshell.

Have you received that Truth in your life? Are you building your life on the foundation of Jesus? When the winds blow, and the storms come to life, will your life hold up under all the pressures? Receive the Good News today and allow Him to take over.

First Step: Confess your sins.

Psalm 51:1-4 David tells us this, "Have mercy on me, O God, according to your unfailing love; according to your great compassion blot out my transgressions. Wash away all my iniquity and cleanse me from my sin. For I know my transgressions and my sin is always before me. Against you, you only, have I sinned and done what is evil in your sight, so that you are proved right when you speak and justified when you judge."

Please take this time to look at your own life. It is always a good thing when we take time to reflect on our hurts, disappointments, fears, and our sins. It is so easy to avoid these topics and live like they do not exist, but it is necessary. When did you last sit down with God and pour your heart out to Him? I encourage you to drop the pretense with God that everything is good. He knows precisely what you are struggling with in your thought life: motives, anger issues, depression, jealousy, and life regrets. David tried his best to cover up his sin but kept getting deeper into the lies.

I encourage you to read Second Samuel 11 and see how David attempted to cover up his adultery with lies and deceit. David thought everything was covered up and under control, but things worsened. His affair leads to murder. Have you ever noticed sin has a way of getting out in the open? Sin will find you out, take you places you never intended to go, and keep you longer than you wanted to stay. Not only does our sin affect us, but it also affects the people around us.

Eventually, David's sin caught up with him. He thought he had pushed it all under the rug, and he thought it had covered it up perfectly. Nobody would ever know, but God was about to bring his sin out in the open.

Second Samuel 12:1-7 tells us, "The Lord sent Nathan to David. When he came to him, he said, 'There were two men in a certain town, one rich and the other poor. The rich man had a very large number of sheep and cattle, but the poor man had nothing except one little ewe lamb he had bought. He raised it and grew up with him and his children. It shared his food, drank from his cup, and slept in his arms. It was like a daughter to him. Now a traveler came to the rich man, but the rich man refrained from taking one of his sheep or cattle to prepare a meal for the traveler who had come to him.' Instead, he took the ewe lamb that belonged to the poor man and prepared it for the one who had come to him. David burned in anger against the man and said to Nathan, 'As surely as the Lord lives, the man who did this deserves to die! He must pay for that lamb four times over because he did such a thing and had no pity.' Then Nathan said to David, 'You are the man!'"

David's sin was exposed! His sin found him out. Look at David's response in verse thirteen. David said, "I have sinned against God."

The reality of his sin slapped him in the face, and he was overwhelmed with guilt and shame. He realized God saw it all. How did David, a man after God's own heart, get here? How did he fall so far? Over time, he built a wall of pride and selfishness, and his heart was full of lust and selfish desires. This wall of sin had affected his relationship with his Heavenly Father. Look what happened in Psalm 51: David realized what he did was wrong and had to be honest with himself and the Lord.

> *Psalm 51:7-12 says, "Clean me with hyssop, and I will be clean; wash me, and I will be whiter than snow. Let me hear joy and gladness; let the bones you have crushed rejoice. Hide your face from my sins and blot out all my iniquity. Create in me a pure heart, O God, and renew a steadfast spirit within me. Do not cast me from your presence or take your Holy Spirit from me. Restore to me the joy of your salvation and grant me a willing spirit, to sustain me."*

David saw his sins, and he turned to the Lord and repented. He cried out to God and asked Him to forgive him and give him a clean heart.

This is where transformation begins by returning to your first love. Ask yourself some serious questions. Where is the passion I once had for Jesus? Where is that desire I used to have for God's Word? What happened to the compassion I once had for other people? When did I start pushing God away and start living for my purposes? It's time to have Psalm 51 conversation with God. It is time to come clean and be open and honest with God.

> *First John 1:9 says, "If we confess our sins, he is faithful and just and will forgive us our sins and purify us from all unrighteousness."*

Stop right where you are and ask God for forgiveness. Confess your sin fully with God and hold nothing back. It is time to dump that heavy load of guilt and sin you have been carrying for years. It is time to lay it at the feet of Jesus. What walls need to come down in your life? Is it that secret sin that has haunted you for years and years? Is it a lustful heart? How about that pride and selfishness? Whatever it is, it can fall if we bring it to the Lord. Lay it at his feet and trust him with it. Then leave it there.

Step Two: Confess Him As Lord.

> *Romans 10:9-13: "That if you confess with your mouth, 'Jesus is Lord,' and believe in your heart that God raised Him from the dead, you will be saved. For it is with your heart that you believe and are justified, and it is with your mouth that you confess and are saved. As the scripture says, 'Anyone who trusts in Him will never be put to shame.' For there is no difference between Jew and Gentile-the same Lord is Lord of all and richly blesses all who calls on Him, for, 'Everyone who calls on the name of the Lord will be saved.'"*

Have you confessed Him as your Lord and Savior? Do you believe that Jesus came to this Earth in the form of a baby and lived the perfect, sinless life? Do you believe He died on a rugged cross and suffered for our sins? Do you believe, three days later, that Jesus came out of that grave and overcame sin and death? Do you believe He is alive and well today and sitting at the right hand of God? If so, it is time to confess it and be ready to tell the world about the wonder-working power of the blood of Jesus. Not only do we need to admit it, but we need to surrender to His Lordship fully. It is time to surrender your will to the will of the Father. Prepare to die to selfishness and pride and live for the King of Glory.

> *Revelations 3:20 says this, "Here I am. Behold I stand at the door and knock. If anyone hears my voice and opens the door, I will come in and eat with him, and he with me."*

Have you answered that knock? Have you given your life to Jesus? Have you told Him thank you for what He has done for you? Have you ever asked him to come in and take over? Here is where it all begins. Answer that knock and open the door to a new life in Jesus. It will be the greatest decision you will ever make. Follow through and become a child of God and experience peace, joy, and happiness.

CHAPTER THREE
WHAT NOW?

W hat a moment! It is an unforgettable experience the moment you ask Jesus into your life. From your heart, the deep acknowledgment that God knows and understands who you are and accepts you into a personal relationship with Him. You said yes to His beckoning, knowing it was the right thing to do in your heart. But it is not unusual to have questions or doubts about your recent decision to receive Jesus as your personal Savior. So many people like you have wondered in the hours or days following this decision about questions like: "What did I do? What does all this mean?

You are not alone. It is more unusual for someone to have no questions or doubts. This decision is a big deal. You just told Jesus you accepted Him and would follow Him all your days. Perhaps you are wondering if it is all real. What about this question: What now? The answers aren't meant to be complicated because God has a way of being profoundly simple. We as people tend to overcomplicate things, especially spiritual things.

We certainly don't have all the answers to every question; however, through the shared experiences of others and truth from the Bible, we can help you find answers to questions like, "What now?" We are excited about your decision to follow Christ and want to come beside you to equip, encourage, and push you close to Jesus. This is an exciting time in your life and the life of this Church. God is on the move, and lives are being changed. The call of the Church isn't just to introduce you to the Lord, but we are called to equip you to be a disciple of Jesus Christ.

We want you to receive this from the beginning: He cares for you, and God loves you.

So please enjoy the ride as you discover and experience your new life in Christ. You just prayed a prayer that has changed your life forever. You ask Jesus to be Lord of your life and ask Him to forgive your sins. He saved you from the consequences of your sins because He willingly paid the price by giving His life in death as a sacrifice for you. This is why it is called salvation. We have been saved from having to pay the price for ourselves. What a powerful prayer. What did I pray that day I received Jesus as my Lord and Savior? Many people call it the sinner prayer. Let's break that prayer down so we can fully understand our commitment.

1. **You admitted you needed Jesus.**

   Romans 3:10-12: "As it is written: 'There is no one righteous, no, not one; There is none who understands; There is none one who seeks after God. They have all turned aside; They have together become unprofitable; There is none who does good, no, not one."

Our human nature is rebellious and opposes God. It causes us to say, "We don't need God." But because of His grace, we can say, "I need God." God offers grace to us so we can admit that we need Him and accept Him. Grace is a gift of God given to help us turn to Jesus and supply us with the power to live for Him.

2. You are willing to turn from your sins.

Jesus said in Mark 1:15: "The time is fulfilled, and the kingdom of God is at hand. Repent and believe in the gospel."'

Repent means turning around to complete a 180-degree turn. That means we are to turn away from a self-centered, self-controlled life. The old way of living is gone; it is time to experience a new life in Jesus.

3. You gave your life to Jesus.

2 Corinthians 5:15: "And He died for all, that those who live should no longer live for themselves, but for Him who died for them and rose again."

You invite Christ to come and live inside of you. You asked Him to come in and take control of your life.

4. You believed that He came into your life and saved you.

John 3:16-18: "For God so loved the world that He gave His only begotten Son, that whoever believes in Him should not perish but have eternal life. For God did not send His Son into the world to condemn the world, but have everlasting life. For God did not send His Son into the world to condemn the world, but that the world through Him might be saved. He who believes in Him is not condemned; but he who does not believe is condemned already, because he has not believed in the name of the only begotten Son of God."

Believing in Jesus means placing your trust in the person of Christ. Therefore, we must learn to trust Him in our daily lives and decisions.

5. You decided to follow Christ in obedience.

John 8:31: "Then Jesus said to those Jews who believed Him, 'If you abide in My word, you are My disciples indeed.'"

God's Word, the Bible, tells us that all people are born into this world as humans separated from a relationship with God. Before you asked Jesus into your life, sin separated us from God. Before sin can be forgiven, according to God's Word, it requires the payment of blood. For many years in the Old Testament, God required an animal's death and the blood to be applied so that human sin could be forgiven. Why is this?

Because sin is not cheap, a cost must be paid to redeem a person from sin, and that price is life-giving blood.

Thankfully, God had enough misuse and knew something more significant was needed. He has always been chasing after a person's heart, not a ritual. He wants a genuine relationship with people, not just repetitive religion. So, God the Father sent Jesus from Heaven to Earth as a human to become the final sacrifice for the sins of all mankind. Jesus died on the cross, and His blood was sacrificed for our sins.

When you ask Jesus to be the Lord of your life and ask Him to forgive your sin, He can save you from the consequences of your sin because Jesus knew no sin and willingly laid down His life on an old, rugged cross as a blood sacrifice for us. This is why it is called salvation. We have been saved from having to pay the price for ourselves. Like any new relationship, it is a process, and there are many things to learn and experience in the coming days. But for now, express yourself to the Lord with a simple, heartfelt prayer and tell Him how much you appreciate what He has done for you. He wants to hear from you.

After you decide to follow Christ, doubt will begin to creep into your mind at some time or another. You may ask yourself: Is this commitment I made with Jesus for real, or did I make a wrong decision? Was I manipulated at an emotional time when my life seemed crumbling around me? How about this question: Why do I still suffer from guilt if I am a Christian? Do I want to do this whole Christian thing? Or perhaps you told a close friend or family member about your decision to follow Jesus, and their response wasn't positive.

> *Jesus said in John 10:10: "The thief does not come except to steal, and to kill, and to destroy. I have come that they may have life and that they may have it more abundantly."*

Jesus didn't come to take anything away from you except sin and your sinful nature. But He came to give you peace and eternal life. But, unfortunately, the thief, the enemy of our souls, wants to steal away life and your belief in what Jesus has done for you. Knowing this, it is no wonder people experience internal doubt, criticism, or fear of what others will think of them after receiving Jesus Christ as their Savior. The dark forces of the enemy don't want you to be confident in your choice; they want to discourage you by any means possible. So when Satan, our spiritual enemy, hits you with doubt, recognize it for what it is: a distraction from the truth. Then, talk with a mature believer who has been a believer for a while. It is always good to seek wise, godly counsel and someone who prays with us.

Living for Jesus doesn't mean everything is going to be perfect. You are beginning your journey, so don't feel pressure to be perfect. Don't forget, there was only one perfect person, and the people hung him on a cross. When living out the Christian life, things may seem unfamiliar, but remember that adjusting to your new life in Christ takes time.

> *Jeremiah 29:11: "For I know the thoughts that I think towards you, says the Lord, thoughts of peace and not evil, to give you a future and a hope."*

Since you have invited Jesus to direct your life as your Lord, you can begin to follow Him and His will instead of doing your own thing or what everyone else thinks you should do. In other words, start following the Father's lead for your life. It will lead you to a life of joy and peace. Moreover, following God's lead will position you for growth and maturity in your new relationship with Jesus Christ.

So many questions always seem to pop up when people are experiencing life change in Jesus Christ. Questions like: Why should I be baptized? Does baptism save you? What does baptism mean, and why is it so important? These are all good questions, so let us give you a simple definition of water baptism. Baptism is an act of obedience when a new believer publicly identifies through the immersion with Jesus' death, burial, and resurrection.

Baptism should be a part of every believer's experience, but it is not a requirement for salvation. Baptism is not merely about being immersed in water, committing, or joining a particular Church. First, baptism is publicly identifying with Christ. Baptism is an outward expression of an inward decision to align oneself with Christ and what He lived and died for. In other words, we get to tell everyone what Christ has done for us and how our relationship with Jesus has changed everything about us.

> *Romans 1:16: "For I am not ashamed of the gospel of Christ, for it is the power of God to salvation for everyone who believes, for the Jew first and also for the Greek."*

> *Luke 9:26: "For whoever is ashamed of Me and My words, of him the Son of Man will be ashamed when He comes in His glory, and in His Father's, and of the holy angels."*

Secondly, water baptism is a picture that carries the weight of cleansing, resurrection, and allegiance. When you are immersed in the water, that symbolizes us dying to the old nature or the old selfish life. Coming out of the water represents us being cleansed from sin and born into a new life in Jesus Christ. Death to the old way of life and resurrection to a new life in Jesus.

The third reason a believer should be water-baptized is that Jesus commanded us to be baptized. Look at what

Jesus said to His disciples when He gave them the Great Commission in Matthew 28:18-20:

> *"All authority in heaven and on earth has been given to me. Therefore, go and make disciples of all nations, baptizing them in the name of the Father and of the Son and of the Holy Spirit and teaching them to obey everything I have commanded you. And surely I am with you always, to the very end of the age."*

Water baptism is also an act of obedience. Think about it this way: Jesus is our ultimate example of how to live life. Would you agree with that statement? I hope so. If Jesus was baptized, do you think we should follow His lead? If that is not enough, baptism also helps us lay down a spiritual marker of remembrance, enabling us to cut out doubt years later. Baptism allows us to reflect on the decisions we made in the past. This obedience act helps us recall this life-changing decision to turn our lives to the Lord Jesus Christ. Last but not least, take a look at Matthew 3:16-17 says this:

> *"When He had been baptized, Jesus came up immediately from the water; and behold, the heavens were opened to Him, and He saw the Spirit of God descending like a dove and alighting upon Him. And suddenly a voice came from heaven, saying, 'This is My beloved Son, in whom I am well pleased.'"*

God was pleased when Jesus was baptized. "Thank you, Jesus, for giving us a good go-by."

CHAPTER FOUR
WHEN WE FUMBLE THE BALL

Your new way of living is just beginning, and you are excited about your future. Getting off on the right foot and going in the right direction is essential. The sooner we understand God's purpose for our lives, the sooner we can fill in the blanks of the unknown questions we may have as new believers. God's first purpose for us to come to Him is because He desires a loving relationship.

> *"Matthew 22:37-38: "Jesus said to them, 'You shall love the Lord your God with all your heart, and with all your soul, and with all your mind.' This is the first and greatest Commandment."*

I grew up loving playing football with my friends in the neighborhood and at school. There was hardly a time when you didn't see a football in my hands. As soon as possible during our summer vacation, I couldn't wait to get outside and gather all our friends. We would play all day and not come in except to eat lunch. Then and only then, my mom forced me to stop and eat. Food was optional at that time in my life. Boy, how times have changed.

Then organized football came into my life. I loved putting on the uniform and the helmet. Playing in real live games was so exciting and so much fun. All the parents would cheer along with family and friends. I loved hearing the sounds of football, the grunts as you were getting hit, the laughter of celebration, and your teammates cheering you on during the game. Game time was so much funnier than practice.

As a kid, I loved playing quarterback. I loved having the ball in my hands. I loved controlling the offense and leading my team down the field. It was so satisfying to score a touchdown and win the game. But as you know, there will always be conflict in football. You will not always be victorious. There will be ups and downs, and you must overcome setbacks and penalties.

I hated to mess up or let my team down. I still remember playing a close game against a friend at my school. We were down a few points, and my team needed to score to win the ball game in the last few minutes. We drove the field and headed down the field to score the winning touchdown. The next play was set for me to take the snap from my center and roll right on a quarterback keeper. It was a good plan because it had worked well for us previously during that game. With a few seconds left, I took the ball from the center, rolled out to the right, and started looking for the closest pathway to the endzone. That endzone was on my site, and I would do anything to score a touchdown. I remember dodging a player and escaping another person's grasp, but the linebacker hit me out of nowhere, and the ball came flying out of my hands. I saw the ball lying on the ground, and both teams attempted to recover the ball. There was a crazy fight for the ball because this was all about winning or losing the game. As the dust settled, the other team recovered the ball. I couldn't believe it; we were close to making a touchdown and winning. But I fumbled. I fumbled at the most critical time of the game.

It is incredible that I still remember that some 43 years later. I remember my sinking feeling when my hands were ripped from the ball. I still see that mental picture of the ball hitting the ground, and there was nothing I could have done to get to it. I still remember the guilt and the shame I felt as the other team celebrated as they ran off the field. That feeling stayed with me for days, mainly because my best friend was on the other team that day. He reminded me daily of his sweet victory when I fumbled the ball.

Here is the truth: We all fumble the ball now and then. We all mess up sooner or later when it comes to living a life for Jesus Christ. We all fall short; we all have regrets and things that we wish we could change from our past. Can you remember the guilt and shame that comes with that mess up? Do you have those that remind you of your past and your shortcomings? Do you run them back over and over again in your mind? How many times have you relived that past decision?

Sometimes, we are spiritually blindsided and knocked off our feet. Sometimes, temptations hit you when you least expect them and cause you to fumble the ball. There will also be those times when we allow our anger and harsh words to slip up and cause hurt feelings, but it is too late to pull them back or recover that relationship that meant so much to us.

Romans 3:23: "All have sinned and come short of the glory of God."

Our relationship with God leads us to fellowship. It is a process of living in daily harmony with God the Father.

Unfortunately, this fellowship can be broken when we allow sin to rule and reign. Sin causes our relationship with God to be hindered, and we can lose communication with the Lord. Guilt and shame will keep us from pursuing a love relationship with Jesus. But there is good news. We must turn to the Heavenly Father when we sin and confess our sins to Him.

> *1 John 1:8-9: "If we say that we have no sin, we deceive ourselves, and the truth is not in us. If we confess our sins, He is faithful and just to forgive us our sins and to cleanse us from all unrighteousness."*

True confession from the heart restores our fellowship with God. Confession acknowledges guilt. It also is the recognition that our sin was against God. Biblical confession requires total honesty with God. We get into trouble when we start trying to cover things up. After you receive Christ, you will continue to repent as you grow in Christian faith and character. True repentance is a change of mind resulting in a shift in behavior. To maintain our fellowship with God, there has to be communication. Communicating with God is called prayer. Prayer was meant to be a two-way conversation. Prayer involves two things: talking and listening. Many of us have the talking part down, but how often do we stop to listen to what God has to say back to us?

Not only does He desire our fellowship, but He also wants us to grow and mature as a child of God.

> *Colossians 1:10: "That you may walk worthy of the Lord, fully pleasing Him, being fruitful in every good work and increasing in the knowledge of God."*

Jesus said in John 10:27: "My sheep hear My voice, and I know them, and they follow Me."

We are called to become more like Jesus. When we become more like Christ, it pleases the Father. It not only pleases God but also brings us joy and fulfillment. We are successful when we are fulfilling our God-given purpose. We must allow the Holy Spirit and the Word of God to remold our words, thoughts, and actions to become more like Christ. Remember, living things always grow.

Satan likes to blindside us and catch us off guard. He wants to strip us of everything important to us or anything we hold dear. Then, the enemy loves celebrating it and keeping it over our heads. He loves to see us living a life of shame and regret. He wants to claim a victory over you and your family. But I want to give you Scriptures of encouragement today that will hold you steady in the game of life.

Ephesians 6:10-11: "Finally, be strong in the Lord and in His mighty power. Put on the full armor of God so that you can take your stand against the devil's schemes."

Joshua 1:6-9: "Be strong and courageous, because you will lead these people to inherit the land I swore to their forefathers to give them. Be strong and very courageous. Be careful to obey all the law my servant Moses gave you; do not turn from it to the right or the left, that you may be successful wherever you go. Do not let this Book of the Law depart from your mouth; meditate on it day and night, so that you may be careful to do everything written in it. Then you will be prosperous. Have I not commanded you? Be strong and courageous. Do not be terrified; do not be discouraged, for the Lord your God will be with you wherever you go."

1 Peter 5:8-11: "Be self-controlled and alert. Your enemy the devil prowls like a roaring lion looking for someone to devour. Resist him, standing firm in the faith, because you know that your brothers throughout the world are undergoing the same kind of suffering. And the God of all grace, who called you to His eternal glory in Christ, after you have suffered a little while, will Himself restore you and make you strong, firm, and steadfast. To Him be the power forever and ever. Amen."

Listen, guys, we will all fumble the ball. In other words, we all mess up along the way. Yes, we sin and have fallen short of what God has called us to be. There has only been One who has lived a perfect life on this Earth, and we crucified Him. But I encourage you to be aware, be ready, and be prepared for Satan's schemes and tricks. Satan doesn't fight fair, and he has no shame. He will throw everything at you, including the kitchen sink.

Chapter Five
Spiritual Checkup

The older I get, the more critical it is to have a yearly check-up with my primary care Doctor. That doesn't include the skin doctor, eye doctor, or dentist. As I type this on my computer, I am finishing up my prep work for my colonoscopy. If you ever had one, you know exactly what I am going through. No words can describe the taste of this nasty liquid we must drink for this procedure. It is unpleasant, but it is necessary to maintain my health and ensure my body is healthy.

I must confess that I am guilty of putting some of these checkups and colonoscopies off as long as possible. Sometimes, I don't want to deal with the truth. At 56 years old, I can't eat everything I want like I did when I was 20. I never had to cut back on potato chips and soft drinks. High cholesterol and blood pressure were words that I couldn't care less about. But I need this accountability to be in touch with my physical body. If something is going on that is not healthy, I need to make changes or take specific steps to a healthy life.

Regarding our physical health, have you ever wondered, "How did we get here?" It seemed like I was healthy and active; the next day, I was fat and out of shape. The change was so gradual that you didn't even notice the change. So many of us put off reality, and we put things off because we don't have the energy to deal with it or the want-to to get things right. We think this: I will do it tomorrow, and tomorrow never comes. In the meantime, your health gets worse and worse. Can anyone relate?

Here is a question I am dying to ask you. When was the last time you had a spiritual checkup? That's right, a spiritual checkup. In other words, when was the last time you got alone with God, dropped your guard, and looked honestly at where you are in your walk with Christ? When did you last ask your Heavenly Father to check out your motives and secret sins? When did you last ask God to shine His spotlight on your thoughts? I understand that sometimes, having a spiritual checkup will not be pleasant, so we put it off or avoid it at all costs. We can deal with it later.

Humor me for a minute or two. What would your graph look like if you could graph your spiritual walk with the Lord over the last ten years? What would that graph tell us about our time alone with God? What would it reveal about your relationship with others? Would your chart look like a rollercoaster with all the ups and downs of life? Would you see a steady growth or a rapid decline?

Where would you be if you could rate your walk with the Lord on a scale of 1-10? One is cold and frigid towards God, and ten is on fire for the Lord. Most men I know would probably say they were a five or a six. That is much better than being at a one or two. Right? But look at what Jesus tells us in Revelation 3:15-16:

> *"I know your deeds, that you are neither cold nor hot. I wish you were either one or the other! So, because you are lukewarm, neither hot nor cold- I am about to spit you out of my mouth."*

In other words, Jesus was saying, "It makes me sick to my stomach to see my children sitting on the fence. Get off the fence and be willing to give me everything." We are all guilty at some time or another when we love to have one foot in the world and the other in the Church. This should not be because that lifestyle doesn't edify the Church.

Why is lukewarm Christianity so dangerous? Think about it this way: imagine a train leaving the station. This train travels just a couple of miles outside of town, and everything seems normal, but just ahead, there is a tree that has fallen across the tracks unknown to the train engineer. The train continued full steam forward and crashed into this massive tree, causing the train to derail. The engine, all the rail cars, and even the caboose came off the track. They were completely derailed, and the destruction was devastating. But it could have been worse. Let me explain.

Now imagine if that train left the station and traveled just a few miles out of town, then hit that tree lying on the tracks, but this time, only half the rail cars came off the track. Now you are asking, how can that be worse than the first situation when all the cars completely derailed? The second situation affects this train and all the trains behind it. It would take days to bring equipment to get those rail cars off the track. Yes, the first situation was horrifying, but being totally off the track allowed other cars to flow and continue on schedule freely.

Living a lukewarm life is dangerous because it affects you and those who are coming behind you. We have to choose who we will follow. Will we surrender to the

Lordship of Jesus Christ, or will we continue living as casual Christians with one foot still in the world?

> *Matthew 16:24-25 Jesus says, "If anyone would come after me, he must deny himself and take up his cross and follow Me. For whoever wants to save his life will lose it, but whoever loses his life for me will find it."*

It is time for action, men; it is time to die to selfishness and pride. It is time to take up the cross of Christ and stop making excuses. It is time to step up to the plate and be the man God has called you to be. It is time to be the godly leader of your household, be the husband who makes Godly decisions, and love your wife the way Christ loved the Church. It is time to stop working so much overtime and spend quality time with your kids. It may be time to set aside a hobby or take your son with you. When did you last take your daughter on a date and listen to her talk about her passions and dreams?

My challenge is to look honestly at your life and get alone with God. Give Him time to examine your heart and your motives. Slow down from your crazy-paced life and step away from the computer, cell phone, and television. When the Lord starts poking and prodding, it may become uncomfortable sometimes but don't run off and hide. But be willing to listen to the prognosis and don't leave without His prescription for healing and fullness. Going to the good Doctor is one thing, but if you don't apply His prescription, it will not do you any good.

> *Lamentations 3:40: "Let us examine our ways and test them, and let us return to the Lord."*

2 Corinthians 13:5: "Examine yourselves to see whether you are in the faith; test yourselves. Do you not realize that Christ Jesus is in you unless, of course, you fail the test?"

Commit to the Lord to get a spiritual checkup. Make an appointment, and be sure to show up. No excuses; this is important and is a must to becoming a better husband and father. It will take time, and it may also cost you. But it will be worth the hassle and discomfort. In this next chapter, I will give you Scripture and some practical direction to help get things right with God. Get ready to take that next step in your walk with Christ. Never forget that it is all about a relationship, not religion.

Notes

Chapter Six
Do Something About It

M en, it is time for action. We all know it is not about sitting on the sideline but stepping up and following God's calling. It is time to lean forward and press on with endurance and passion. It is time to stop all the spiritual whining and rise to the occasion. We are caught up in a spiritual war and unprepared for battle. Paul was a man of action. He was always the first to step in and take the lead or speak a difficult word. I love what Paul shares in Philippians 3:10-14:

"I want to know Christ and the power of His resurrection and the fellowship of sharing in His sufferings, becoming like Him in His death, and so, somehow, to attain the resurrection from the dead. Not that I have obtained all this, or have already been made perfect, but I press on to take hold of that which Christ Jesus took hold of me. Brothers, I do not consider myself yet to have taken hold of it. But one thing I do: Forgetting what is behind and straining toward what is ahead. I press on toward the goal to win the prize for which God has called me in heavenward in Christ Jesus."

Paul said, "I have not arrived, and I still have some work to do regarding knowing Christ. But I am giving it my all." He persevered and pushed through difficulties to become like His Savior. He pushed aside his past failures and shortcomings and kept moving forward to win the prize of Jesus Christ. What a great example he gives us to follow when pursuing Christ. Men, we have a race to run! Not only are we called to run the race, but we are called to win the prize. Participating is not enough, but we have to go all in. We need to give it everything we have for the glory of God. Look at what the writer of Hebrews tells us in Hebrews 12:1-2:

> *"Therefore, since we are surrounded by such a great cloud of witnesses, let us throw off everything that hinders and the sin that so easily entangles, and let us run with perseverance the race marked out for us. Let us fix our eyes on Jesus, the author and perfecter of our faith, who for the joy set before Him endured the cross, scorning its shame, and sat down at the right hand of the throne of God."*

If we are going to run to win, we have to throw off everything that hinders us in our love relationship with Christ. We are to throw off lust and shame from our hearts and fix our eyes on the very One who hung the sun into orbit. We have to keep our eyes on the end goal of knowing Jesus. What is it that is hindering your walk with Jesus today? What continues to trip you up and cause you to stumble and fall? What distractions does Satan use on you over and over again? Let's look at Colossians and see what Paul tells us to do to live a victorious Christian life.

> *Colossians 3:5-10: "Put to death, therefore, whatever belongs to your earthly nature: sexual immorality, impurity, lust, evil desires, and greed, which is idolatry. Because of these, the wrath of God is coming. You used to walk in these ways, in the life you once lived. But now you must rid yourselves of all such things such as these: anger, rage, malice, slander, and filthy language from your lips. Do not lie*

to each other, since you have taken off your old self with its practices and have put on the new self, which is being renewed in knowledge in the image of its Creator."

In other words, we need to put off our old ways of living. It is like mowing the lawn in the dead of summer. After you cut the grass, weed eats, edge, and blow everything off; you get dirty from head to toe. I cannot tell you how many times I had had to rinse off at an outside faucet and strip down in the garage before I entered the clean house. You guys know what I am talking about.

Similarly, in the spiritual realm, we are sinful and covered in sin and selfishness. Before entering the Lord's presence, we must wash off and put off the nastiness of sin and shame. We need to come clean before His throne of grace. We must put off anger, rage, malice, slander, lust, and filthy language. We need spiritual cleansing. I want to give you ten easy steps that will help you do that. Yes, there are ten practical things we can do to get things right with our Heavenly Father. All you need is thirty minutes, a willingness to hear the Lord, and the guts to follow through with obedience.

There is nothing as messy and aggravating as a clogged drain, especially the sinks in the bathroom. Over time, different things fall into the sink and find their way down the drain. The collection of objects builds up, clogs the drain, and stops the water flow. Because of the build-up, the water begins to back up in the sink. Then you jump into action and grab the Drano, clothes hanger, or whatever you think will free the blockage. All we want is for the water to flow through the drain again.

Here is my question: How is the flow of the Spirit in your life? Is there sin clogging up the spiritual drain and not allowing the flow of God to move in your life? The greatest hindrance to the flow of God isn't a problem of motivation but one of accumulation. Christians often experience frustration and defeat in their spiritual lives due to a nasty buildup of unconfessed sin.

> First John 1:9: "If we confess our sins, He is faithful and just to forgive our sins and to cleanse us from all unrighteousness."

Unconfessed sin blocks God's flow and movement in our lives, but confession is the tool we need to free up our spiritual drain and end our frustration and aggravation. We need a good spiritual cleaning and experience freedom and joy again in our relationship with Jesus. I encourage you to follow this simple ten-step spiritual cleansing process and not rush through it.

1. **Find a quiet place to sit alone for at least one hour with a sheet of paper, something to write with, and your Bible.**

2. **Quiet your heart before the Lord by sitting still. Leave your phone in another room and push aside all distractions.**

3. **Pray to the Lord and thank Him for bringing you to this place. Let the Lord know you are committed to getting your heart right with Him and unclogging your spiritual drain.**

4. **Ask Him to reveal your sins one by one.**

5. Begin to list everything the Holy Spirit reveals to you. Don't ignore the difficult ones.

6. Confess your sins one at a time to the Lord. Go through your list no matter how many sins you have listed. Tell Him how sorry you are, and ask Him to forgive and cleanse you.

7. Anticipate the personal struggle you will face. Fight the desire to run away and forget this whole process.

8. Make restoration wherever necessary and expect to humble yourself to at least one person.

9. Write done on your paper. Receive His forgiveness and grace. Yes, say it out loud to your Heavenly Father.

10. Thank the Lord for forgiving and showing you so much grace. Thank Him for cleansing your spiritual drain and allowing the flow of the Spirit to move in your life once again. Praise Him for His endless love, and enjoy His fellowship.

A spiritual oil change is necessary if we commit to being yoked with Christ. If we are faithful to Christ's calling, we must first put off everything that hinders us or holds us back from fully serving our Heavenly Father. We need to confess our sins and ask for forgiveness. But we can't stop there, or we will fall short of what God calls us to do. After we release our sins, our shortcomings, and all our failures, get ready to receive His grace, His mercy, and all of His goodness. In other words, put off those things that hinder our relationship with the Lord and put on the things of Christ. Complete the total spiritual oil change and continuously watch your next appointment because it is not a one-time appointment.

Put to death or put off anything that hinders our walk with Christ. Confess our sins to a Holy God and ask Him to cleanse us from all unrighteousness. Paul didn't stop there, but he went on to say this in Colossians 3:10-14:

> *"Put on the new self, which is being renewed in knowledge in the image of its Creator. Here there is no Greek or Jew, circumcised or uncircumcised, barbarian, Scythian, slave or free, but Christ is all and is in all. Therefore, as God's chosen people, holy and dearly loved clothe yourselves with compassion, kindness, humility, gentleness, and patience. Bear with each other and forgive whatever grievances you may have against one another. Forgive as the Lord forgave you. And over all these virtues put on love, which binds them all together in perfect unity."*

Put on compassion, kindness, humility, gentleness, and patience. But top it all off with love to the proper levels. Unyoke from the things of this world that bog you down and make your work for Christ hard to complete. Unyoke from sin, depression, and anxiety. Then make sure to yoke to the things of God that will direct your attention to Christ Himself. Then look how Paul wraps this truth up in Colossians 3:15-17:

> *"Let the peace of Christ rule in your hearts, since as members of one body you were called to peace. And*

be thankful. Let the word of Christ dwell in you richly as you teach and admonish each one another with all wisdom, and as you sing spiritual songs with gratitude in your hearts to God. And whatever you do, whether in word or deep, do it all in the name of the Lord Jesus, giving thanks to God the Father through him."

Let the peace of God rule your heart. In the presence of God, you will find rest and peace that only comes from Him. You will find comfort in His yoke even when things are falling apart. His yoke will give us direction and purpose for our life. He doesn't leave you alone, but He is with us every step of the way. He will help you carry that heavy load that is too heavy for you. It is not what we bring to the table, but it's all about what we are willing to surrender to our Heavenly Father. Can you say today, "Lord, I surrender all?"

Dennis L Taylor

Notes

CHAPTER SEVEN
SATAN'S STRATEGY

Nothing is more exciting as a pastor than seeing a grown man humble himself before the Lord, confess his sins, and give his heart to the King of kings. That is what I call Kingdom work. Even the angels in Heaven celebrate and rejoice over that one changed life. To that new believer in Christ, he is experiencing the freedom of being in Christ and having his sins forgiven. He has become a child of God and is high-stepping because he now has eternal life. No more guilt, regret, and shame. He praises the Lord, and everyone celebrates his decision to surrender everything to Jesus. But their journey is just beginning!

Men of God know that Satan is ticked off. He has lost you for all eternity, but he will do everything in his power to cause you heartache and grief. The Bible tells us that Satan has come to kill, steal, and destroy. He is good at what he does, and he has no shame. The enemy doesn't play fair and doesn't mind hitting you when you least expect it. Satan has a strategy, and he is very tactical with his attack. The excitement of your new life in Christ disappears, and the reality of life settles in. Then, we must figure out how we apply Jesus to our everyday lives. Life can get crazy, and the pressures of temptation do not go away; they may even intensify. Can any of you testify?

We love the Lord, but many dedicated Christian men have difficulty living victorious lives. We get caught up in the agony of bondage and sin. Spiritually, we get bound up in a stronghold of selfishness and pride. A stronghold doesn't go away until we fully submit to the Lordship of Jesus Christ.

> *Ephesians 6:10-12: "Finally, be strong in the Lord and in His mighty power. Put on the full armor of God so that you can take your stand against the devil's schemes. For our struggle is not against flesh and blood, but against the rulers, against the authorities, against the powers of this dark world, and the spiritual forces of evil in the heavenly realms."*

Here is the truth: God loves you and has a beautiful plan for your life. Satan hates you and has a destructive scheme for you and your family. Satan is a deceiver and a liar. He is the great tempter of man, trying his best to trip you up and cause you heartache. Satan is brash and full of himself. He wants to fill you with helplessness and make you feel defeated. The enemy masquerades as an angel of light and a servant of righteousness. He was kicked out of Heaven and sent to Earth, and now he wants to do everything he can to cause us grief.

But Jesus had a different mission to complete. Let's take a look at Luke 4:18 and see why Jesus came to Earth:

> *"The Spirit of the Lord is on Me because He has anointed me to preach the good news to the poor, He has sent me to proclaim freedom for the prisoners and recovery of sight for the blind, to release the oppressed, to proclaim the year of the Lord's favor."*
>
> *1 John 3:8: "He who does what is sinful is of the devil because the devil has been sinning from the*

beginning. The reason the Son of God appeared was to destroy the devil's work."

Here is my question: Upon whom are you going to depend on? It seems like a no-brainer, right? But how often do we make dumb decisions that are not according to what God has called us to do and be? How many times have we pulled away from the truth because we listened to the lies of Satan? If you depend on God, He will give you victory. It may not be overnight, but keep focused on His promises and wait for the Lord.

> *James 5:7-9: "Be patient, then, brothers, until the Lord's coming. See how the farmer waits for the land to yield its valuable crop and how patient he is for the autumn and spring rains. You too, be patient and stand firm, because the Lord's coming is near. Don't grumble against each other, brothers, or you will be judged. The Judge is standing at the door."*

Satan will do his best to make us impatient and irritate us as much as possible. He doesn't want us to consult the Lord and seek His guidance. The enemy loves to see us under pressure, upset, and rushing to make a rash decision. That is how he operates; he wants to come into your house, tie you up with rope and chains, and take over your household. That should tick you off! Look at what Jesus said in Matthew 12:29:

> *"How can anyone enter a strong man's house and carry off his possessions unless he first ties up the strong man? Then he can rob his house."*

A couple of years ago, when we were living in Georgia, my house was broken into during the middle of the day. Laura came off from lunch, just like always. She opened the garage and entered the house. Laura noticed glass on the floor as she walked into the kitchen to make herself a sandwich. She thought it strange, but our dog had knocked something off the shelf. So she called out to our dog but did not respond, which was strange. Then Laura began to look around, and our back door stood wide open. As she began to look around the kitchen, she noticed our window had been busted out. Then it hit her: someone had broken into our house. She glanced toward our bedroom and noticed our bed had been flipped and our room was destroyed. So she ran back out of the garage and called me. At the time, I was eating a sandwich for lunch at my desk at work. My phone rang, and I saw it was Laura calling. So, I picked up my phone to answer her but could not understand what she was saying. I remember telling her to take a deep breath and slow down. Finally, she calmed down enough to tell me what just happened. I tried to stay calm, but instance fear hit my body. So many thoughts flooded my mind, but I told her to hang up and call 911. I left work and headed straight home, where Laura talked with the police outside our house.

I will never forget that feeling of helplessness and anger. I know that is an odd combination of emotions, but I was so upset that some stranger could come into my house and take anything they wanted that I have worked so hard to provide for my family. I felt violated. That day, Laura and I decided to get a house alarm system. It would be worth the money to have some sense of security again. At that point, I would do almost anything to keep unwanted guests out and protect what I hold dear.

Satan doesn't hesitate to break into your life and take what is not his. He loves to see us hurt and leave you in a sense of helplessness. The enemy will steal from you without blinking an eye. He wants to rob you of your joy, peace, and passion for life. He will rob you of relationships such as your wife, family, or closest friends. He will not have any feelings of guilt or remorse. He loves to cause pain and suffering. His thinking is that He is bound for Hell, and that will not change, so why not take as many people with him as possible? That is his strategy. He has a plan, and he will cause as much pain and suffering as he can with the time he has.

What precautions are you taking to protect your family from Satan's attacks and schemes? Do you know the authority you have as a believer in Christ Jesus? Look at what Paul shares with us in Colossians 2:13-15:

> *"When you were dead in your sins and in the uncircumcision of your sinful nature, God made you alive with Christ. He forgave us all our sins, having canceled the written code, with its regulations, that was against us and that stood opposed to us; He took it away, nailing it to the cross. And having disarmed the powers and authorities, He made a public spectacle of them, triumphing over them by the cross."*

Through a personal relationship with Jesus, we are made alive in Christ. Our sins were forgiven, and the laws and regulations were canceled. We can live a victorious Christian life because of Jesus' victory over sin and death. Christ has disarmed the powers and authorities of this world. He has made a spectacle of them and given us authority because of Christ in us. Christ has come to free us from the bondage of fear and death. Jesus came to destroy the works of the devil.

Satan has many different names and powers. He is a deceiver, tempter, accuser, and the Angel of Light. The enemy condemns, destroys, controls, and wants to bring wrath upon you as a man. But he hates that Jesus has given us authority over him and his demons because of the blood of Christ. So, he will do anything to doubt our salvation and to cause us to get tripped up in sin. Satan will give us excuses to walk in disobedience and plant seeds of unforgiveness in our hearts. He will creep in through the tiniest opening he can find and steal from you. Sin keeps us from having the authority and power of God in our lives. That is Satan's plan; that is his scheme. He wants to disarm you as a man of God and tie you up with addictions, pornography, adultery, and lust.

Men, it is time to break free from the devil's schemes! It is time to confront the sin in our lives and remove the shackles of bondage. We are men of God, and we can have authority over Satan and his schemes. Don't back down, and get ready to fight! Look at what Paul says in Ephesians 6:10-13:

> *"Finally, be strong in the Lord and in His mighty power. Put on the armor of God so that you can take your stand against the devil's schemes. For our struggles is not against flesh and blood, but against the rulers, against authorities, against the powers of this dark world, and against the spiritual forces of evil in heavenly realms. Therefore put on the full armor of*

God so that when the day of the evil comes, you may be able to stand your ground."

Are you ready to stand? Are you prepared to fight back? Have you had enough of being beaten down, walked on, and tripped up by Satan's tricks and temptations? Enough is enough. It is time to do something about it. It is time to break free and regain our authority in Jesus Christ. What stronghold needs to be broken in your life?

Notes

CHAPTER EIGHT
MY NEW IDENTITY IN CHRIST

In Christ, we have a new identity. Take time today to soak that in because we can start fresh in this life. In Jesus, we are set free from bondage and sin. He is the giver of life and wants to elevate you as a man. He wants to promote you as a husband and a dad. He cares about your day-to-day worries and troubles. He gives us everything we need to live a victorious Christian life and is right there at our side, cheering us on. So rise up, you men of God, and live a life that will bring glory to the name of our Heavenly Father. Look at what Paul tells us in Colossians 1:10-14:

"And we pray this in order that you may live a life worthy of the Lord and may please Him in every way: bearing fruit in every good work, growing in the knowledge of God, being strengthened with all power according to His glorious might so that you may have great endurance and patience, and joyfully giving thanks to the Father, who has qualified you to share in the inheritance of the saints in the kingdom of light. For He has rescued us from the dominion of darkness and brought us into the kingdom of the Son He loves, in whom we have redemption, the forgiveness of sin."

Because of Christ's work in us, we should bear good fruit, increase the knowledge of God, and become steadfast in our faith. Joy should flow from our lives and good works from our hands. Little by little, we should be becoming more like Him. Inch by inch, moving closer to the heart of the Heavenly Father. Yes, we have a new identity in Christ Jesus. The old is gone, and the new has come. We are to walk in a manner worthy of the Lord. Let's dive into God's Word to see the Scripture that backs this up.

> *2 Corinthians 5:17-21: "Therefore, if anyone is in Christ, he is a new creation; the old has gone, the new has come! All this is from God, who reconciled us to Himself through Christ and gave us the ministry of reconciliation: that God was reconciling the world to Himself in Christ, not counting men's sins against them. And He has committed to us the message of reconciliation. We are therefore Christ's ambassadors, as though God were making His appeal through us. We implore you on Christ's behalf: Be reconciled to God. God made Him who had no sin to be sin for us so that in Him we might become the righteousness of God."*

> *Ephesians 1:7-8: "In Him, we have redemption through His blood, the forgiveness of sin, in accordance with the riches of God's grace the He lavished on us with all wisdom and understanding."*

> *1 Corinthians 6:9-11: "Do you not know that the wicked will not inherit the kingdom of God? Do not be deceived: Neither the sexually immoral nor the idolaters nor adulterers nor male prostitutes nor homosexual offenders nor thieves nor the greedy nor drunkards nor slanders nor swindlers will inherit the kingdom of God. And that is what some of you were. But you were washed, sanctified, and justified in the name of the Lord Jesus Christ and by the Spirit of our God."*

Romans 8:5-11: "Those who live according to the sinful nature have their minds set on what that nature desires; but those who in accordance with the Spirit have their minds set on what the Spirit desires. The mind of sinful man is death, but the mind controlled by the Spirit is life and peace; the sinful mind is hostile to God. It does not submit to God's law, nor can it do so. Those controlled by the sinful nature cannot please God. You, however, are controlled not by the sinful nature but by the Spirit, if the Spirit of God lives in you. And if anyone does not have the Spirit of Christ, he does not belong to Christ. But if Christ is in you, your body is dead because of sin, yet your spirit is alive because of righteousness. And if the Spirit of Him who raised Jesus from the dead is living in you, He who raised Christ from the dead will also give life to your mortal bodies through His Spirit, who lives in you."

Galatians 3:13-14: "Christ redeemed us from the curse of the law by becoming a curse for us, for it is written: 'Curse is everyone who is hung on a tree.' He redeemed us in order that the blessing given to Abraham might come to the Gentile through Christ Jesus so that by faith we might receive the promise of the Spirit."

Colossians 3:1-10: "Since then, you have been raised with Christ, set your hearts on things above, where Christ is seated at the right hand of God. Set your mind on things above, not on earthly things. For you died, and your life is now hidden with Christ in God. When Christ, who is your life, appears, then you also will appear with Him in glory. Put to death, therefore, whatever belongs to your earthly nature: sexual immorality, impurity, lust, evil desires, and greed, which is idolatry. Because of these, the wrath of God is coming. You used to walk in these ways, in the life you once lived. But not you must rid yourselves of all such things as these: anger, rage, malice, slander, and filthy language from your lips. Do not lie to each other, since you have taken off your old self with its practices and have put on the new self, which is being renewed in knowledge in the image of its Creator."

This is straight out of the Word of God. This is not just an opinion or my thoughts but a message to men straight out of the Bible. These are words to live by that can change your direction in life and set you free from worldly thinking. Listen, if you are in Christ Jesus and the Holy Spirit lives in you, you have a new identity. You have been set free by the blood of Jesus, and you are now the Children of God. You have been freed from sin and death. Put away the old way of living, put off anger, lustful thoughts, coarse jokes, and selfish living. Put on the things of God that will bring Him glory and honor. With your new identity comes a new way of thinking. With a new way of thinking comes a new way of living. A new way of living comes with a new purpose in life. Your life will not be centered around you but in Christ Jesus. Your new identity in Christ will change the way you think about yourself. Allow me to give you a few examples of how to change your thinking:

Instead of thinking I am unworthy or unacceptable. Know that you are accepted and worthy. (Romans 15:7; Psalm 139:13-24)

If you feel like a failure, know you are adequate in Christ. (1 Corinthians 3:5-6; Philippians 4:13)

If you are fearful and anxious, you can be freed from fear and worry. (Psalm 34:4; 2 Timothy 1:7; 1 Peter 5:7; 1 John 4:18)

You may think of yourself as weak and feeble, but you are a mighty warrior in Christ. (Daniel 11:32; Psalm 37:39; Philippians 4:19)

Maybe you feel dumb and not that smart; know that you have the wisdom of God available to you. (Proverbs 2:6-7; 1 Corinthian 1:30; James 1:5)

Instead of thinking I am in chains and living in bondage, you can know you are free in Christ. (Psalm 32:7; 2 Corinthians 3:17; John 8:36; Isaiah 40:9-16)

If you feel unloved, know you are loved and adored. (John 15:9; Romans 8:35-39; Ephesians 2:4, 5:1; 1 John 4:10-11)

You may feel unworthy and don't fit in anywhere; know that the God of the universe has adopted you. (Romans 8:16-17; Galatians 1:14,20; Ephesians 1:5, 1 John 3:2)

Do you ever feel guilty? In Christ, you are forgiven. (Psalm 103:12; Ephesians 1:7; Colossians 1:14,20; Hebrews 10:17)

If you are depressed and hopeless, you will have all the hope you will ever need in Christ. (Romans 15:13; Psalm 16:11, 27:13, 31:24)

You may feel defeated and beat up, yet with your new identity, you can be victorious. (Romans 8:37; 2 Corinthians 2:14; 1 John 5:4)

If you feel God is so far away, you can experience His closeness because of what Jesus did for us. (Ephesians 2:6; 1 Peter 2:5-9; Matthew 6:14-15)

> *1 John 3:1-3: "How great is the love the Father has lavished on us, that we should be called children of God! And that is what we are! The world does not know us because it did not know Him. Dear friends, now we are children of God, and what we will be has not yet been made known. But we know that when He appears, we shall be like Him, for we shall see Him as He is. Everyone who has this hope in Him purifies himself, just as He is pure."*

Since we are a new creation in Christ, we must stop saying, "I have anxiety." You may be anxious, have many concerns, or be stressed out. But stop putting a possessive around something the devil wants you to have. In other words, stop speaking words the devil wants you to say about yourself. Yes, the enemy is coming after you, and the flesh is trying to drag you down. But if you are in Christ, you have the power of the Holy Spirit inside of you. You have experienced victory because of the blood of Jesus Christ! Start owning what God wants you to own, and reject what the devil wants to stick on you. It is a new way of thinking. It's a new way of living. We have a new identity in Jesus!

CHAPTER NINE
YOUR TIME ALONE WITH GOD

W hat is your highest priority in life? What would you say is the most important thing in your life? What is one thing in your life you cannot do without? How will you answer that question?

Our greatest priority in life should be our time alone with God. Do you mean that time alone with God is more important than that job that puts food on my table and a roof over my head? Or more important than my wife and children? Yes, your time with God should be your highest priority because your time alone with God will make you a better employee, husband, and father. Starting your day with the God of the universe will give you the wisdom and discernment you need to make good decisions and walk in righteousness throughout the day. Look at what David said in Psalm 27:1-5:

> *"The Lord is my light and my salvation-whom shall I fear? The Lord is the stronghold of my life whom shall I be afraid? When evil men advance against me to devour flesh, when my enemies and my foes attack me, they will stumble and fall. Though an army besieges me, my heart will not fear; though a war breaks against me, even then will I be confident. One thing I ask of the Lord, this is what I seek: that I may dwell in the house of the Lord all the days of my life, to gaze upon the beauty of the Lord and to seek Him in His temple. For in the day of trouble and will keep*

me safe in His dwelling; He will hide me in the shelter of His tabernacle and set me high upon a rock."

David faced difficult times during his reign as king and had many enemies. Yes, he had plenty to worry about and so much to lose. But David's time alone with God was his stronghold and high tower. His time with God is where he found His safety and his rest. It was no secret what David held most important in his life. My time alone with God has carried through thirty-seven years of marriage and thirty-five years of ministry. God has grown, corrected, stretched, and made me more like Christ.

Many of you know what a time alone with God is all about, but some are asking what is a quiet time with God and why I need to do this every day. First, let's cover what a time alone with God is. We set aside time to talk and listen to our Heavenly Father. It is a time we carve out of our day to give God our undivided attention. Most Christians would say that spending time with God would be a great habit to develop, but most do not make their quiet time a priority. It is puzzling to me, but I am speaking the truth. Maybe you have been encouraged to develop this discipline, but no one has ever walked you through the whys and the hows of meeting with God. And in your frustration, you stopped because it just didn't make sense to keep spinning your wheels, and it seemed to be going nowhere.

> *Luke 5:15-16: "Yet the news about Him spread all the more so that crowds of people came to hear Him and to be healed of their sickness. But Jesus often withdrew to lonely places and prayed."*

If meeting with the Father was important to Jesus, shouldn't it be essential to us? As busy as Jesus was, as overwhelmed as He must have felt, He still withdrew to pray. Jesus withdrew to a quiet place to be alone with the Father. In those quiet, intimate times, Jesus gathered the strength He would need to accomplish the task God had called Him to. By escaping the noise of the day, Jesus provided us with an excellent illustration for us to follow today.

Spending time with God daily moves us from a religious approach to God to a more relational approach. Where there is no communication, there is no relationship. Where there is no relationship, there is no trust. The less you trust someone, the harder it is to follow someone. A person without quiet time is most likely struggling with unresolved issues and unconfessed sins.

The Word of God is one of the centerpieces needed when hearing the Lord. Ask the Lord to give you a desire to read and understand His anointed Word. Be willing to apply His truth to your life and allow it to go deep into your soul. A quiet time with the Lord deepens our walk with the One who seeks our friendship the most. Take time daily to enjoy being in the presence of God, and continue to seek His face and not His hands. Here is a great prayer to open up with your time alone with God.

Psalm 119: 33-40: "Teach me, O Lord, to follow your decrees; then I will keep them to the end. Give me understanding, and I will keep your law and obey it with all my heart. Direct me in the path of your commands, for there I find delight. Turn my heart toward your statutes and not toward selfish gain. Turn my eyes away from worthless things; preserve my life according to your word. Fulfill your promise to your servant so that you may be feared. Take away the disgrace I dread, for your laws are good. How I long for your precepts? Preserve my life in your righteousness."

I enjoy my time alone with the Lord, but it hasn't always been that way. There have been seasons when I struggled to have a consistent time alone with the Lord. Even though I faltered occasionally, I kept pushing forward and discovered a few things that helped me along the way.

First, I scheduled my time alone with God. That's right. It was just like a Doctor's appointment; I blocked out a time to meet with the God of the universe. If I didn't, it would have never happened. I find mornings are best for me. I now enjoy getting up and starting my day with Jesus. I love getting into God's Word and taking the time to hear from God. It is the best way to start your day and set the mode for the rest of the day. Second, choose a place. Get away from all distractions. Yes, that means televisions, cell phones, and other people. Be creative and make that place special. Choose a location off the beaten path, away from daily activities. Establishing this quiet place to get alone with the Father is so important.

Thirdly, come up with a plan and stick with it. Set a period for how long you commit to meeting with God. With this period, how long do you spend in prayer? How many minutes do you open up the Word of God? How much time do you pause and be still to hear the voice of the Lord? Whatever the plan is, work at it, but don't get caught up in it and get stuck in a routine. Keep it as fresh as possible.

If you long to be that Christian man who stood faithful for decades, you have to be willing to follow through with this commitment to meeting with the Lord. We will find wisdom, strength, and endurance alone with the Lord.

Dennis L Taylor

Notes

CHAPTER TEN
A CALL TO MEN TO SERVE

What is our attitude when it comes to serving others? Serving others is not a glamorous thing to do. We usually want to be served and look out for number one. Please take a look at all the people we respect and look up to. Most of them are self-serving, and it is all about them. It is all about what they want and how they like nice things. Why is being a servant so attractive in today's society? Think about it this way: Jesus was a servant to the people, and we are called to be just like Him. So, how do we grow to be like Jesus? How do we go from wanting to be served to a man that serves those around us? It is not easy, but I want to give you four steps to take to be more like Christ when it comes to serving others.

First step: We have to go from selfishness to servanthood.

John 13:1-5: "It was just before the Passover Feast. Jesus knew that the time had come for Him to leave this world and go to the Father. Having loved His own who were in the world, He now showed them the full extent of His love. The evening meal was being served, and the devil had already prompted Judas Iscariot, son of Simon, to betray Jesus. Jesus knew that the Father had put all things under His power, and that, He had come from God and was returning to God; so He got up from the meal, took off His outer clothing, and wrapped a towel around His waist. After that, He poured water into a basin and began to wash

His disciple's feet, drying them with the towel that was wrapped around Him."

The very Son of God humbled Himself, became a servant, and washed His disciple's feet. It should have been the other way around. His disciples should have washed Jesus' feet. How often, as men, do we do things to draw attention to ourselves, even in our Churches? Yes, we may volunteer and do many good things, but our motives are not pure and pleasing to the Lord. We all need to hear the truth: God will not move and work where there is pride. When pride pops up, it's in our hearts; God will remove His hands from you, a Church, or a ministry. So how did Jesus do it? How did He stay so grounded and humbly serve others?

Jesus had the right relationship with God. He stayed close to the Father's heart. He spent time with the Heavenly Father in prayer and close communion. Jesus also had the right relationship with the people around Him. He loved people, and He cared for their needs. Our Lord not only saw their needs but met those needs with righteous service. Last, Jesus was secure with who He was and what God called Him to do. Only a confident man can serve. I never want to be a pastor who can't scrub a toilet. I challenge you to take steps away from selfishness and step into servanthood. What does that look like for you? What is God saying to you about your willingness to serve? Please, don't allow pride to sneak in and take control of your heart.

James 4:10: "Humble yourself before the Lord, and He will lift you up."

Second step: Go from talking to walking.

Anybody can talk a big game. How often have we heard guys talk about how good they could play a particular sport, and they go on and on about what they did in High School? They fill the air with how many points they scored in middle school basketball and how fast they ran in high school. Then, they couldn't chew gum and walk simultaneously when it came down to it. They were full of a lot of hot air. They did a lot of talking but couldn't back it up with their actions. Do our words back up what we are saying we believe? Jesus gives us a practical example of how to stop talking about serving and start living it out.

We must leave our comfort zone when walking out of our faith and serving others. We need to get comfortable with being uncomfortable. Jesus saw a need, and He met that need. In John chapter thirteen, no one at the table wanted to stop eating and wash everyone's feet. Can you imagine how dirty these men's feet were? They wore sandals, and they mostly walked on dirt roads everywhere they went. We were talking about some severe toe jam. Jesus didn't have to form a committee. He didn't have to get an official title or a corner office at the local synagogue. He didn't have to have it approved at the monthly business meeting. As uncomfortable as it was, Jesus washed His disciple's feet.

If we go from talking to walking out our faith, we must learn to lay aside whatever hinders us. Verse four tells us that Jesus took off His outer clothing and wrapped a towel around His waist. In other words, He got everything out of the way that would hinder Him from serving His disciples by washing their feet. Here is my question to you: what is hindering you from serving those people around you? What's in your way of serving those who are hurting and alone? It is time to put our faith into action. It is time to step up and back up our talk.

What can we, as men, do to back up our talk about our faith? Let me give you a few little ideas. Ask the Lord to provide you with people's names that might need encouragement, then write them a handwritten note and send it in the mail. It may be a friendly text to let them know you are thinking about them. Invite a friend to grab a coffee, pay for it, and ask them how they are doing. Encourage them, pray for them, and find ways to encourage them throughout the week. Set aside time each week to spread hope and love.

Step three: Move from pride to humility.

John 13:6-10: "He came to Simon Peter, who said to Him, 'Lord, are you going to wash my feet?' Jesus replied, 'You do not realize now what I am doing, but later you will understand.' 'No,' said Peter, 'you shall never wash my feet.' Jesus answered, 'Unless I wash you, you have no part with me.' 'Then, Lord,' Simon Peter replied, 'not just my feet but my hands and my head as well. Jesus answered, "A person who has had a bath needs only to wash his feet; his whole body is clean. And you are clean, though not every one of you."

Pride is a disease that makes everyone sick but the one who has it. Peter was reluctant and resistant to Jesus' leading. Pride has a way of leading us astray and pushing us down the wrong road. Pride will also destroy us, our relationships, ministry, and our family.

Proverbs 16:18-19: "Pride goes before destruction, a haughty spirit before a fall. Better to be lowly in spirit and among the oppressed than to share plunder with the proud."

Proverbs 18:12: "Before his downfall a man's heart is proud, but humility comes before honor."

Proverbs 11:2: "When pride comes, then comes disgrace, but with humility comes wisdom."

Men of God, run to humility. Be aware of the trap of pride that Satan places in a strategic place in our lives. Yes, a carefully designed plan to serve a particular purpose or advantage. Satan is a liar and a thief; he will do anything to hurt, destroy, and accuse you.

Step four: Move from fear to freedom.

John 13:13-17: "You call me 'Teacher' and 'Lord,' and rightly so, for that is what I am. Now that I, your Lord and Teacher, have washed your feet, you also should wash one another's feet. I have set you an example that you should do as I have done for you. I tell you the truth, no servant is greater than his master, nor is the messenger greater than the one who sent him. Now that you know these things, you will be blessed if you do them."

Jesus said, "Follow my lead." That was His clear message to us even today. It sounds easy and makes sense, but sometimes we have fears in our spirit. Let's be realistic: what are our fears regarding being a servant and following Jesus' lead? Do you ever feel like people will take advantage of or make fun of you? Do you think the Lord will ask us to do something that will make us uncomfortable or beyond our capabilities? Fear is a liar and wants to rob us of the joy of living the Lord and serving His Church. Men of God set fear aside and walk in the freedom found in a close personal relationship with Jesus Christ.

> *2 Corinthians 3:16-17: "But whenever anyone turns to the Lord, the veil is taken away. Now the Lord is the Spirit, and where the Spirit of the Lord is, there is freedom."*

Because the Spirit of Christ lives in us as believers, we can experience freedom from fear and what people think of us. The "old man" is gone, and the "new man" has come. The old way of thinking is a thing of the past. A new way of thinking has arrived and will make a difference in how we live and the questions we may ask the Lord instead of asking the Lord what the Church has for my family and me. You will begin to ask, what can I do for His Church? How can I serve You, Lord?

Rise up, O men of God. It is time to serve others. Men of God, stand to your feet and get ready to serve those people around you and love them to Jesus Christ. It is time to serve unselfishly and put on the attitude of servanthood. Yes, it is time to humble ourselves before the Lord and do those things not many people are willing to do. It is time to stop talking a good game and put action on our faith and the words we speak. Lay aside whatever is hindering you or holding you back. Be willing to be honest before the Lord, and don't be scared to ask Him for help and encouragement. Set aside that selfish pride that desires all the attention and seeks to receive the credit. Run after humility and seek

God's face more than His hands. Last, it is time to go from fear to freedom. Be willing to follow God's lead. Be the man that God has called you to be. Lead in a way that will bring glory and honor to the God of the universe.

Whatever the Lord has put in you, do it with all your heart. Give it your very best and follow Jesus' example of how He served others so unselfishly. Be willing to open your spiritual eyes to see those around you who are in need and are struggling. Step out of that comfort zone and expect God to work in and through you. To God be the glory forever and ever! Amen.

Notes

CHAPTER ELEVEN
PURSING THE HOLINESS OF GOD

1 Peter 1:13-16: "Therefore, prepare your minds for action; be self-controlled; set your hope fully on the grace to be given you when Jesus Christ is revealed. As obedient children, do not conform to the evil desires you had when you lived in ignorance. But just as He who called you is holy, so be holy in all you do; for it is written: 'Be holy, because I am holy.'"

God has given every born-again man a command to live a holy life. Not only to the pastors, missionaries, or teachers. This calling to holiness was given to you if you have placed your faith in Jesus Christ. Many Christian men have what I call a cultural holiness, where they adapt to the Christians around them. You see, God has called us to be like our pastor. He hasn't called us to be like the godliest man you know, but He has called us to pursue a holiness that is evident in His life. I encourage you to consider it: what does that mean for my life? How would this thought affect how we talk, handle difficult situations, or what we do on Friday nights?

1 John 1:5-7: "This is a message we have heard from Him and declare to you: God is light; in Him there is no darkness at all. If we claim to have fellowship with Him yet walk in darkness, we lie and do not live by truth. But if we walk in the light, as He is in the light, we have fellowship with one another, and the blood of Jesus, His Son, purifies us from all sin."

God is free from evil, and His ways are completely pure. So, what about us? How does our life compare with His? Does that throw you for a loop? Does this call to holiness seem unattainable and way beyond our reach? Does that overwhelm you as a believer in Christ Jesus? How can we, as men, live a life acceptable to the Lord with that standard? God knows what we face daily and the amount of temptation around us, right?

I assure you, Jesus knows exactly what we face on Earth. He knows how Satan can tempt, lie, and deceive us. Jesus knows how Satan can take the truth and twist it around to make us stumble and fall. Pursuing holiness is a process. Yes, it does take time, but we first must acknowledge His Holiness. One way of doing that is to take time to praise Him. In other words, we turn our focus off ourselves and turn our eyes to the Lord. That is where it all begins, but we know that God demands more; acknowledging His holiness, He told us to be holy. It didn't sound optional to me; He demanded it.

Let me pause here for a second or two: Have you ever tried to justify your actions with God, which our conscience calls into question? Have we made excuses for our continual pattern of sin or tried our best to cover up the areas we struggle with when it comes to sin? Here is where we make statements like I am still growing in that area of my life, God understands. I will use some strong words here, so brace yourself: God doesn't accept our excuses for sinning! Sin breaks our fellowship with the Lord, and He will not put up with it as a Holy Father. He loves us too much to let it slide. Take a look at the writer of Hebrews in chapter 12:7-11:

"Endure hardship as discipline; God is treating you as sons. For what son is not disciplined by his father? If you are not disciplined (and everyone undergoes discipline), then you are illegitimate children and not true sons. Moreover, we have all had human fathers who disciplined us, and we respected them for it. How much more should we submit to the Father of our spirits and lives? Our fathers disciplined us for a little while as they thought best, but God disciplines us for our good, that we may share in His holiness. No discipline seems pleasant at the time, but painful. Later on, however, it produces a harvest of righteousness and peace for those who have been trained by it."

God desires that we grow in holiness, in the righteousness of God. Yes, we all fall short and sin but stop making excuses for sitting in the same place of continual sin. It is the trap of Satan, and God loves us too much to allow us to sit there. He will disciple us, get our attention, and do whatever it takes to move us from that spot of disobedience. It may be painful, and it may not be pleasant at that time, but it will be what brings us righteousness and peace.

I cannot tell you how often my Earthly father had to correct me. His favorite verse had to that one that says, "Spare the rod, spoil the child." Some days, I remember getting two or three spankings a day. I was a slow learner but realized he would not allow me to act out. I didn't appreciate it then, but now I am so thankful he didn't let me walk in disobedience. Look at Hebrews 12:14:

"Make every effort to live in peace with all men and to be holy; without holiness, no one will see the Lord."

Because God is holy, He hates sin. I know hate is a strong word, but it perfectly explains how God feels about our shortcomings and mess-ups. Think about it: we do something God hates every time we sin. As we grow in holiness, we, too, will grow to hate sin. When we take our eyes off Christ, we grow accustomed to our sin and the sin around us. In other words, we adapt to the world and its ways. But God never ceases to hate evil.

> *1 Peter 1:17: "Since you call on a Father who judges each man's work impartially, live your lives as strangers here in reverent fear."*

God doesn't hate sin in one person and overlook it in another. He judges each of us impartially. Look at David's life; he was a man after God's own heart. God anointed him as king over Israel and blessed him with many things. Yet, David fell into sin and committed adultery with Bathsheba, and then he had her husband killed to hide his sin. Even though God loved David, the Lord had to grab his attention and punish him to correct his wrongs. God exposed David's sins. Look at what the Lord said to David in 2 Samuel 12:11-12:

> *"Out of your own household, I am going to bring calamity upon you. Before your very eyes, I will take your wives and give them to one who is very close to you, and he will lie with your wives in broad daylight before all Israel."*

Even King David was corrected when he got off track. God doesn't overlook our sins and sweep them under the carpet; He loves us way too much to do that. The Father corrects us as sons. Yes, His Holiness is a high standard, but it is nevertheless a standard that He holds us to. Men, it is time for us to grow in holiness and seek God's face. We are responsible for leading our families and teaching our kids God's ways. Our family's success depends on it, and God demands it. This is not an option.

Is there something you need to get right with God? Is there a sin you need to confess? Is there an attitude you need to get right? Is there someone you need to go to and get things right with? Is there an old habit you need to let go or run from?

> *Romans 6:11-14: "In the same way, count yourselves dead to sin but alive to God in Christ Jesus. Therefore do not let sin reign in your mortal body so that you obey its evil desires. Do not offer the parts of your body to sin, as instruments of wickedness, but rather offer yourselves to God, as those who have been brought from death to life; and offer the parts of your body to Him as instruments of righteousness. For sin shall not be your master, because you are not under law, but under grace."*

> *1 Corinthians 6:18-20: "Flee from sexual immorality. All other sins a man commits are outside his body, but he who sins sexually sins against his own body. Do you not know that your body is a temple of the Holy Spirit, who is in you, whom you have received from God? You are not your own; you were bought at a price. Therefore honor God with your body."*

Men, let's make our Heavenly Father proud. Let us run the race in such a way as to bring glory to the Father. Flee from pornography, sexual immorality, and anything that breaks our fellowship with the Father. Let us chase after the things of God and pursue holiness and righteousness. Confess your sins, run from the evils of this world, and walk in purity.

CHAPTER TWELVE
FROM EXISTING TO REALLY LIVING

I have a question that I want you to think about for a few minutes. Are you really living life, or are you just existing? In other words, are you doing exactly what God has called you to, or are you just trying to get by and survive this life? If you were anything like me, you would say, "I am doing fine, nothing to jump up and down about, but I am good."

For many years, I went to Church every time the doors opened. I taught Sunday School, served as a Deacon, and served on several committees. On the outside, I seemed to be living the perfect Christian life. Yes, I was saved, no doubt about it. But I was content to stay exactly where I have been spiritually for several years. I didn't care to move from my spot. You could say I was in a spiritual rut and very comfortable there.

I had a great job at Bell South, a beautiful family, a beautiful wife and daughters, and we just built our two-story dream home. It was everything I ever wanted in life, but something was missing. Have you ever had the feeling that there has to be more? Yes, there had to be more to life than this. But I was telling God I was only going so far in my faith walk with Him because I didn't want to risk what I had in my Earthly hands.

As I headed to work early one morning, I prayed to God; I finally came clean with my Heavenly Father. I laid it all on the line and admitted I was in a spiritual rut, sick and tired of this mundane Christian life. I was tired of living safely and never fully trusting Him with my life. That morning, I told the Lord I would give Him everything, no matter the cost. Yes, I finally told Him, "I surrender all!." Then, the tears flowed down my face, and I drove to work. A few moments went by, and it hit me. What did I pray? I couldn't believe those words just came out of my mouth. It felt so good, but I never knew what He would teach me. I would be changed forever.

Maybe you are in a spiritual rut? Are you just going through the motions of Church life? You may work one hundred miles an hour in the Church but see very little life change. It took me a long time to learn that it is not doing but more about who you are in Christ. It is not about who you are, but it is all about whose you are. The Lord seeks someone willing to seek Him no matter the cost and ready to run into His presence.

> *1 Samuel 16:7: "But the Lord said to Samuel, 'Do not consider his appearance or his height, for I have rejected him. The Lord does not look at the things man looks at. Man looks at the outward appearance, but the Lord looks at the heart.'"*

My question is: What does God see when He looks at your heart? How big is your want to? In other words, how big is your desire to be like Christ? Are you tired of the same old, same old? I want to encourage you to do three things to help you go from existing to living.

1. Be honest with the Lord and converse honestly with Him.

Tell Him you are tired of just existing and want to live life with purpose and passion. Tell Him you are ready to take a leap of faith and hold nothing back from Him. Be willing to surrender everything and trust Him with your greatest treasures. Yes, it is time to be real with your Heavenly Father and get everything off your chest.

What's stopping you from saying those words? Is it fear? Is it the fear of the unknown, or maybe it's doubt? Perhaps you wonder if you step out on that limb, will God catch me if I fall? Self will do everything it can before it will die. Self will sing in the choir, and it will gladly sing a solo, too. Self will teach, and it will also preach a great sermon every Sunday. Now, we come to our second step if we want to go from existing to really living.

2. Self has to die.

Galatians 2:20: "I have been crucified with Christ, and I no longer live, but Christ lives in me. The life I live the body, I live by faith in the Son of God who loved me and gave Himself for me."

Let this verse come alive in you. Before you invited Christ to come into your heart, self-ruled upon the throne of your heart. What self-wanted, self-went after and took it, and there were no issues. But when Christ took the throne of your heart, things changed. But we must understand that our selfish ways and wants didn't disappear or leave our physical bodies. They still exist, and they are still with us, and the selfish is battling for the throne of our hearts. Self will do whatever it takes to rule our hearts once again. Take a look at Ephesians 6:12:

"For our struggle is not against flesh and blood, but against the rulers, against authorities, against the powers of this dark world, and against the spiritual forces of evil in heavenly realms."

Romans 6:8-11: "Now if we died with Christ, we believe that we will also live with Him. For we know that since Christ was raised from the dead, He cannot die again; death no longer has mastery over Him. The death He died, He died to sin once and for all; but the life He lives, He lives to God."

Because of what Jesus did for us on the cross, we can experience life. You see, not only did He overcome sin, but He also overcame death. Yes, we, too, can experience the same victory because of the power of the blood of Jesus. Sin cannot hold us, self can't control us, and death has no say in our lives! It is time to put selfishness and pride aside. It is time to die to self and run after the things of God. Look at what Colossians 3:5–8 tells us:

"Put to death, therefore, whatever belongs to your earthly nature; sexual immorality, impurity, lust, evil desires, and greed, which is idolatry. Because of these, the wrath of God is coming. You used to walk in these ways, in the life you once lived. But now you must rid yourselves of all such things as these: anger, rage, malice, slander, and filthy language from your lips. Do not lie to each other since you have taken off your old self with its practices."

Yes, put to death whatever belongs to the old man. Put off selfishness and pride. Electrocute everything that doesn't please the Lord. But we can't stop there; after we strip our lives of all the things that are not of God, we need to put on everything God says is necessary for our daily lives. Let's continue in Colossians and see what Paul is trying to tell us.

> *Colossians 3:10-14: "Put on the new self, which is being renewed in knowledge in the image of the Creator. Here there is no Greek or Jew, circumcised or uncircumcised, barbarian, Scythian, slave or free, but Christ is all and is in all. Therefore, as God's chosen people, holy and dearly loved, clothe yourselves with compassion, kindness, humility, gentleness, and patience. Bear with each other and forgive whatever grievances you may have against one another. Forgive as the Lord forgave you. And over all these virtues put on love, which binds them all together in perfect unity."*

Men, let's fill our minds with the things of God. Beware of what you allow to dominate your time, what you think, and what you receive from the world and its influence. Commit to the Lord today to pursue His heart, ways, and presence. This leads us to the third thing: we must go from existing to living for Christ.

3. We must be full of the Holy Spirit.

> *John 7:37-39: "On the last and greatest day of the Feast, Jesus stood and said in a loud voice, 'If anyone is thirsty, let him come and drink. Whoever believes in Me, as the Scripture has said, streams of living water will flow from within him.'"*

I want to bring out a couple of words that we need to look at and focus on when it comes to being full of the Spirit.

The first word that jumps out in this verse is thirst. As men of God, we need an intense desire for more of God's things, including the Holy Spirit. We must desire Him more than we desire sports or our hobbies. We must want Him more than shooting a big buck or catching a fish to mount on the mantle of our fireplace.

I remember playing High School football back in 1984; I know, it was so long ago. But we were going through a summer camp in full pads. We didn't have the privilege of getting water every fifteen minutes. We have one chance to get water during a two-hour practice. Our source for water didn't come from a cooler with your cup. I wish it would have been like that, but it wasn't. We had to drink from a water hose hooked to a PVC pipe. Holes were drilled every sixteen inches down this long pipe. My first thought was I would never drink from something like that. Especially if someone else has put their mouth over the hole I had to drink from. It reminded me of cows going to drink water from a trough. But in ninety-degree weather in full pads, I remember standing in line to suck the water out of that PVC pipe, and I didn't care who had their mouth on it before me. In other words, I intensely desired to get to the water and drink it. Do we have an intense desire for more of the Holy Spirit?

The second term that sticks out to me in these verses is when Jesus said, "Come and drink." Come and Drink speaks about participation and receiving of the Holy Spirit. If you will, can you imagine God sending us a Heavenly straw from Heaven to Earth to fill us with everything we need to help us grow and be strengthened? Then, we must believe that what we have received is God's best and His anointing. Don't just rely on feelings or emotions, but genuinely believe.

If we as men of God can thirst for the Holy Spirit, open up our hearts and souls to receive and participate in the works of God, and believe in our hearts that the Holy Spirit lives inside of us, then the streams of living water will flow from our lives and into the lives of people around us. Then, we will see timid men become bold. Quiet men will become vocal, and greedy men will become generous.

You see, God has called us to be containers. Yes, we are the temple where the Holy Spirit dwells. If you are alive in Christ, you have the Holy Spirit living inside of you. But here is my question? What kind of container are you? Do you have the right lid on, or do you have a significant leak? Or are you full of the Holy Spirit and ready to fulfill your life purpose and passions? God wants us to be full of the Holy Spirit and desires to stay topped off and ready to go.

Men, we have to run the race to win. It is not enough to show up at the starting line. It is time to go from existing to really living. But let me tell you, it may cost you, will take effort, and will consume much of your energy. But it will all be worth it. He wants to bring us all to a place of total dependence on Christ. It is time to seek His face more than we seek His hands.

God's singular purpose is to make us like His Son Jesus. Our relationship with Jesus should affect our attitudes, actions, and affections. I said all this in the hope that you can experience more joy in your worship, more power in your prayers, and more success over your struggles. I also pray that you can have more joy and victory in your faith walk in Christ.

There is so much more to life than just getting by. There is so much to this life than going to work, eating, sleeping, and doing it all over again. It is time to really live, but make sure to have a real honest talk with the Lord, die to selfishness and pride, and be full of the Holy Spirit. Get ready to live your best life. It is found in a love relationship with Jesus.

CHAPTER THIRTEEN
IT'S TIME

So many people are worried about the extinction of sea turtles, bald eagles, and elephants. But to tell you the truth, I am more concerned about the end of a godly man who knows how to live a holy life and lead his family and the Church of Jesus Christ. Whether we realize it or not, war has been declared on the family and the sacred estate of marriage.

One out of every two marriages ends in divorce. One million teenagers will become pregnant out of wedlock in one year. Abortion has gone crazy, and doctors don't blink an eye at killing our precious babies. Sixty-six percent of all Church-involved teenagers are sexually active. Can you imagine the percentage of unchurched teenagers? Also, every 80 seconds, a teenager in America attempts suicide. Can we say that Satan is alive and well in our world today?

Let me ask you something: as a man, what are you doing to keep your marriage off the casualty list? Too often, we have the attitude that will never happen to us. Satan doesn't discriminate just because you are a leader in your Church. If anything, he will turn up the heat for any leader in our Churches nationwide. While I have you thinking, let me ask you another question. What are you doing to keep your kids off that same casualty list? I am not asking what the mom or the grandparents are doing. I am asking you, as a dad, what are you doing to protect your kids from the schemes of Satan himself?

As a Student Pastor for many years, I cannot tell you how many parents came to me begging me to do something with their children. They would be in tears, saying, "Please tell them about Jesus; I am at the end of my rope." Men of God, it is not the youth pastor's job to tell your children about Jesus. Yes, they are to come alongside and help, but that is your responsibility as a man of God.

Time is slipping away fast. I remember when I could hold my two girls like a football; they are grown and married and living their best lives. Where did the time go? How did they grow up so fast, and how did we get so old? We have to make our time on this Earth count. Here is another question: What will you leave behind when you are dead and gone? What will people say about your faith and the legacy of how you lived your life?

The enemy cannot kill the family without dividing the husband and the wife. That is where he puts his efforts, and it is working. It is called divide and conquer. As men of God, we need to recognize the devil's schemes and not fall to his lies and deceit. Satan knows if he can destroy the Christian families, he can significantly neutralize the Church of Jesus Christ. Men of God, it is time to wake up from our spiritual slumber. It is time to stop playing games. It is time to take ourselves from our hearts' throne and place our relationship with Jesus as our number one priority. Man up, fall to your knees, and pray like never before. Open the Word of God and dive into the truths and promises found in this inspired Word. Let's tell the world about the amazing grace of our Heavenly Father. It is time for men to lead our families and Churches well. It is time to shake the gates of hell and step away from contentment and spiritual laziness. It is time to take the gloves off and stand up for what we believe. Get off the fence and stop living just like the world.

You may be asking, "How do I fight for my family?" First, make Jesus your number priority and spend quality time talking and listening to His voice. Hide His Word in your heart and share it with as many people as possible. Secondly, invest time and money into your relationship with your wife. Never stop dating her, and tell her how much you love her. Then, love on your kids. Our kids spell love, T-I-M-E. Make sure to do all the little things that will leave a lasting impression on their hearts. Go outside and play ball, ride bikes, build a tree house, and even have a tea party with your daughter.

How often are we guilty of saying, "I don't have time; I am so busy." Take it from me as a dad with grown children; time will pass you by. We, as dads, better make time because it may cost you a child on the causality list. Has hunting, fishing, and other hobbies with the guys taken up all your family time? Satan is no fool; he knows exactly what he is doing. When the devil wants to destroy a family, in most cases, he focuses on the man.

I want to warn you that when a man gets serious about following Jesus, prepare for the shelling to start. He will throw everything he can at you, even the kitchen sink. Get ready for temptation to hit a new level in your life. He wants to frustrate you, discourage you, and do everything he can to overwhelm you and give up. Prepare yourself and get ready for the battle. Stay focused on Christ and lean on Him for strength.

We will all say, "I am willing to do whatever it takes to protect my family. I am willing to die for them." That is well and good, but what families need today is for the dads to be willing to live in Christ and reflect His love to my family. Dads, let's live for our families; rise up and be the men God has called us to be.

> *Ephesians 5:25-26: "Husbands, love your wives, just as Christ loved the church and gave Himself up for her to make her holy, cleansing her by the washing with water through the word."*

That is a huge challenge; we must love our bride as Christ loves us. I will not pretend I have it all together, but I have learned a lot from my thirty-seven-year marriage. Yes, I learned from my mistakes, most of the time. We need to be intentional when nurturing our relationship with our wives. Sometimes, we must think outside the box and go the extra mile. My goodness sake, do not forget those birthdays, anniversaries, and special occasions! Being a godly husband will not be easy, but it is possible. Hang in there, guys; you may have been knocked to the canvas, but get back up and be willing to fight! It is so worth it. Be ready to ask yourself those difficult questions like: Am I doing everything I need to do to be Christ to my wife?

> *Ephesians 6:4: "Fathers, do not exasperate your children; instead, bring them up in the training and instruction of the Lord."*

That verse is easy to read but hard to put into real life. To defeat a prominent opponent, we have to have a good plan. Raising godly children takes commitment, determination, and the heart of a warrior. We, as men, have to be willing to put into practice what we profess. In other words, we must be authentic, transparent, and sold out to the Word of the Lord. Our children need to see us praying, reading our Bibles, and sharing the love of Christ. Today's kids need a godly example for living this crazy life.

It's time! One man can make a difference. You can impact your family, church, and your friend group. We can do all things through Christ; that gives us strength.

Notes

CHAPTER FOURTEEN
THE CALL OF THE ORDINARY

What kind of man does God choose to do His work? Have you ever stopped long enough to think about that? Think about it: Jesus had this huge task He wanted to accomplish; He tried to spread the Gospel worldwide, baptize them, and disciple them. That task is complex, with so many moving pieces and details to work out. Indeed, he would recruit some of the top students in their higher education ranks. He went all over the region looking for men with unique gifts and talents. These men had to be well off and have substantial funds to travel and assist Jesus in the impossible task. But Jesus had a different way of thinking. Take a look at 1 Corinthians 1:6-9:

> *"Brothers, think of what you were when you were called. Not many of you were wise by human standards; not many were influential; not many were of noble birth. But God chose the foolish things of the world to shame the wise; God chose the weak things of the world to shame the strong. He chose the lowly things of this world and the despised things-and the things that are not-to nullify the things that are, so that no one may boast before Him."*

Jesus became incredibly popular among the people of Galilee. He worked many miracles and taught like no other man. He spoke with great wisdom and authority. Everyone knew there was something special about this Jesus. Everywhere Jesus went, the multitude followed Him, waiting for the next miracle or profound word. But when the crowd reached their peak, Jesus began preaching bolder messages confronting sin and false teaching. Then, many of the bystanders started to fade away. Take a quick look at John 6:66-69:

> *"From this time many of His disciples turned back and no longer followed Him. 'You do not want to leave too, do you?' Jesus asked the Twelve. Simon Peter answered Him, 'Lord, to whom shall we go? You have the words of eternal life. We believe and know that you are the Holy One of God.'"*

As you see, the original Twelve stayed with Christ for the moment. These were the men that Jesus personally chose to fulfill His mission here on Earth. These were the Twelve whom Jesus shared with one-on-one and discussed intimate details with. Yes, Jesus called each man to leave everything to follow Him. In other words, He called them to salvation and to walk with Him daily. Then Jesus called this ordinary group of guys to ministry. Look at how Jesus extended His call to Peter and Andrew in Matthew 4:18-20:

> *"As Jesus was walking beside the Sea of Galilee, He saw two brothers, Simon called Peter, and his brother Andrew. They were casting a net into the lake, for they were fishermen. 'Come, follow me,' Jesus said, 'and I will make you fishers of men.' At once, they left their nets and followed Him."*

Instead of fishing for fish, Jesus called His disciples to be fishers of men. This is what I call a different direction in life. This was radical; fishing was all they had known since they were little boys. Wouldn't you think they would have asked some questions before they committed to embark on this journey with Jesus? Not only did Jesus call them to ministry, but He also called them to Apostleship. Look at Mark 6:7-10 and see how Jesus instructed the Twelve to reach out to people around them:

> *"Calling the Twelve to Him, He sent them out two by two and gave them authority over evil spirits. These were His instructions: 'Take nothing for the journey except a staff-no bread, no bag, no money in your belts. Wear sandals but not an extra tunic. Whoever you enter a house, stay there until you leave that town. And if any place will not welcome you or listen to you, shake the dust off your feet when you leave, as a testimony against them."*

Jesus sent them out two by two. He probably noticed they were not quite ready to go out alone. The Twelve disciples played a massive role in spreading the Gospel of Jesus and planting Churches worldwide. Most of the Twelve were killed for the cause. With all that has been said about these men, we would all agree they should be highly esteemed for their willingness and guts. They were great men of God, and they impacted history. But I want to notice something: Jesus didn't choose a rabbi, scribe, pharisee, or priest. They were not seminary trained, just fishermen, tax collectors, and everyday ordinary men. The Twelve were people, just like many of us. Look at what was said about Peter and John in Acts 4:13:

> *"When they saw the courage of Peter and John and realized that they were unschooled, ordinary men, they were astonished, and they took note that these men had been with Jesus."*

These ordinary, blue-collared workers turned the world upside down in Jesus' name. It wasn't because of their excellent education, unlimited resources, popularity, or stunning looks. But it was the surrendered life of men who willingly left everything to follow Jesus' command. God did excellent work in them to accomplish this great task. Yes, Jesus chooses the humble, available, and meek of this world to confuse the wise.

> *1 Corinthians 1:20-21: "Where is the wise man? Where is the scholar? Where is the philosopher of this age? Has not God made foolish the wisdom of the world? For since in the wisdom of God the world through its wisdom did not know Him, God was pleased through the foolishness of what was preached to save those who believed."*

I am sure Jesus had some interesting times with the Twelve, just like He does with us. Getting these ordinary men to become world changers couldn't have been easy. They were, at times, selfish, self-absorbed, and proud. Look at what happens in Matthew 9:33-35:

> *"They came to Capernaum. When He was in the house, He asked them. 'What were you arguing about on the road.' But they kept quiet because, on the way, they had argued about who was the greatest. Sitting down, Jesus called the Twelve and said, 'If anyone wants to be first, he must be the very last and the servant of all.'"*

Not only were they selfish, but they were hardheaded, foolish, and slow to believe. Now, they are beginning to sound a lot like us. Now remember, this was Jesus' first stringers! Do you ever wonder if Jesus wanted to redraft and start again and pick an entirely different group of guys? The original Twelve also lacked faith; there were four times in the New Testament when Jesus said to them, "You of little faith." Look at scripture found in Matthew 8:23-26:

> "Then He got into the boat, and His disciples followed Him. Without warning, a furious storm came up on the lake, so the waves swept over the boat. But Jesus was sleeping. The disciples went and woke Him up, saying, 'Lord, save us! We're going to drown. He replied, 'You of little faith, why are you so afraid.'"

Have you ever wondered what Jesus saw in these guys? Story after story, we see the Twelve displaying a lack of commitment, lack of power, and even the lack of faith. No one could ever look at this group of guys and conclude they turn the world upside down with their abilities and commitment. If we were honest with each other, we could probably see ourselves in the Twelve and genuinely relate to them. If Jesus could use these guys to turn the world upside down, He can surely use us. We seem to have a lot of the same character traits. Look what Paul says about our weaknesses and shortcomings in 2 Corinthians 12:7-10:

> "To keep me from becoming conceited because of these surpassingly great revelations, there was given me a thorn in my flesh, a messenger of Satan, to torment me. Three times, I pleaded with the Lord to take it away from me. But he said to me, 'My grace is sufficient for you, for my power is made perfect in weakness.' Therefore I will boast all the more gladly

about my weakness, so that Christ's power may rest on me. That is why, for Christ's sake, I delight in weaknesses, in insults, in hardship, in persecutions, in difficulties. For when I am weak, then I am strong."

There you have it, guys. God loves to use ordinary men to do extraordinary things. We may not be the sharpest pencil in the stake, but that will not stop us. We may lack special skills and little money, but His grace is sufficient for me, and His power is perfect in our weakness. Dream big, men of God, but make sure you pray bigger. Make sure to say yes to Jesus and be willing to give up everything to follow Him. Let's change our world, one soul at a time. Let's turn this world upside down again.

CHAPTER FIFTEEN
MAN UP, LET'S GO

Matthew 28:18-19: "Then Jesus came to them and said, 'All authority in heaven and on earth has been given to me. Therefore go and make disciples of all nations, baptizing them in the name of the Father and of the Son and of the Holy Spirit, and teaching them to obey everything I have commanded you. And surely I am with you always, to the very end of the age."

What do we believe? Do we believe that Jesus is the Son of God? Do we believe that He is the light of the world? Do we believe Jesus is the King of kings and the Lord of lords? Do we believe He is the source of hope, joy, and true happiness? Do we believe that He is in control? Do we believe He can make a difference in people's hearts? Then why is the Church so quiet? Why aren't we shouting it from the rooftops?

Men, we have been quiet long enough! It is time to take it off cruise control and for the Church of Jesus Christ to sound the alarm. I pray that God will open our spiritual eyes to see as He sees. "Shake us up, Lord, disturb us and our busy schedules. Stir up in us a spirit of urgency, a spirit of compassion, and a fresh spirit of love within Your Church.

The Heavenly Father has issued a command here in Matthew twenty-eight. Notice something: this is not known as the Great Suggestion. Instead, it is called the Great

Commission. He is calling us to go. We have done enough sitting in our chair. We are called to go into a lost and dying world and love people. We are to build relationships and serve the people. We are called to go and give away His love to those who are hurting, lost, and those who are empty and searching for purpose in life.

Have you ever stopped and taken a good look at the world that we are living in? Have you stopped and looked at your local newscast and seen all the chaos that is going on all around us? Broken homes are at an all-time high. Sickness and disease tear this world apart in several ways. Satan is on the attack, and He will not ease up. He is determined to cause as much destruction as possible before being handcuffed and thrown into hell forever. In the meantime, he is doing everything he can to cause us grief.

Men of God, it is time to engage our hearts and hands. It is time to put into action what we believe. It's time to get our hands dirty and love people to Jesus Christ. Look at the example that Jesus gave us in Matthew 9:35-36:

> *"Jesus went through all the towns and villages, teaching in their synagogues, preaching the good news of the kingdom, and healing every disease and sickness. When he saw the crowds, he had compassion on them because they were harassed and helpless, like sheep without a shepherd."*

Jesus went outside the four walls of the Church building and loved on people. He was full of compassion, and He felt their pain and suffering. But look at what Jesus has to say to us in Matthew 9:37-38:

"The harvest is plentiful, but the workers are few. Ask the Lord of the harvest, therefore, to send out workers into his harvest field."

Jesus is calling us to a grander vision of living. Saying yes to God's grandeur vision of living is saying yes to people. I encourage you to slow down long enough to see what is eternal and temporary. What are you investing in that will fade away and crumble one day? Are you investing in people's souls who will spend eternity in hell or Heaven? We need to see that Jesus loved people. He genuinely cared for people.

Jesus is calling the world to Himself. He calls them to come as they are, for the Kingdom of God is open to them. A grander vision of living is looking through the eyes of Christ and seeing people who do not know Jesus and seeing their potential once they receive God's love and power. What would happen in our Churches if we were passionate about carrying out the Great Commission? What would happen in our cities and prisons nationwide if the Church of the living God would put on the eyes of Christ and share our testimony? Can you imagine how our school systems would be different?

I must confess that I love seeing born-again men of God catching the vision of reaching out to people for Christ. I especially enjoy hearing that one of them has led someone to Christ for the first time. But even more than this, I love seeing a few infectious Christian men spread the germ to others in their fellowship. Who in turn pass it on to more people until an evangelistic epidemic erupts throughout the Church. If God can so effectively use one contagious Christian, what will happen when the whole Church becomes contagious? When that happens, the entire community will have an explosive spiritual impact.

I don't have to tell you that most Churches aren't like that yet. Far too many times, Churches are trying to retain their membership, meet the budget, and maintain the status quo, with no real vision for reaching the lost. The truth is that dying Churches are focused on membership. In that case, the Church is irrelevant. When the Church is inwardly focused, they become self-serving and ask what it does for them.

> *Matthew 16:13-18: "When Jesus came to the region of Caesarea Philippi, he asked his disciples, 'Who do people say the Son of Man is?' They replied, 'Some say John the Baptist; others say Elijah; and still others, Jeremiah or one of the prophets.' 'But what about you?' he asked. 'Who do you say I am?' Simon Peter answered, 'You are the Christ, the Son of the living God.' Jesus replied, 'Blessed are you, Simon son of Jonah, for this was not revealed to you by man but by my Father in heaven. And I tell you that you are Peter, and on this rock, I will build my church, and the gates of Hades will not overcome it.'"*

Jesus was talking about building a Church that the gates of hell couldn't overcome. His vision of the Church would be active and on the move. His Church would be dynamic and all about life change. It will be an expanding force to be reckoned with. Jesus's mission for the Church was to rescue, redeem, and recruit people mired in sin. We have a tremendous job ahead of us and must be on guard against complacency. People need the Lord, and God has given us the commission to share the Truth of Jesus with this lost and dying world.

Sharing Christ can be as simple as starting a conversation; just a few ordinary Spirit-guided steps can have a life-changing impact on the people around you. Think about it this way: Jesus walked out of Heaven and wrapped Himself in human flesh. Then he stretched out His hands on a rugged cross to save us from our sins and the penalty of eternal damnation.

> *Romans 5:6-8: "And hope doesn't disappoint us, because God has poured out his love into our hearts by the Holy Spirit, whom he has given us. You see, at just the right time, when we were still powerless, Christ died for the ungodly. Very rarely will anyone for a righteous man, though for a good man, someone might possibly dare to die. But God demonstrates his own love for us in this: While we were still sinners, Christ died for us."*

What an amazing love! Christ extracted Himself from the ultimate circle of comfort to step across time and space to rescue us. Look at Paul's word in Philippians 2:6-8:

> *"Your attitude should be the same as that of Christ Jesus: Who being in the very nature of God, did not consider equality with God something to be grasped, but made himself nothing, taking the very nature of a servant, being made in human likeness. And being found in appearance as a man, he humbled himself and became obedient to death, even death on a cross!"*

Men, it is time to humble ourselves and rid ourselves of selfish pride. It is time to live by faith and not by sight. It is time to care for people and extend ourselves to our community. It is time to sow and water the seed of love with prayer. It is time to share the Good News of Jesus Christ and follow the nudging of the Holy Spirit in our lives. It is time to reach out and be a channel of God's great love. The time is now! Complacency has no place in the Church. It's time to get to the starting line. On your marks, get set, and go!

CHAPTER SIXTEEN
CLOSING THOUGHTS ON
ACCOUNTABILITY

I wish I could type words that would stir up a heart of passion in every man, pushing them closer to Christ. I hope I can nudge each of you to spend time alone with God daily and let the world see the difference Christ will make if He is sitting on the throne of their heart. I pray over you, the reader, to be the man God has called you to be. I pray you will be that loving husband that goes beyond what you should do. I pray over you wisdom and strength that all comes from the Creator of Heaven and Earth. I encourage you to be that godly dad who pours into your children and grandchildren. Dive into the Word of God, hit your knees, and pray like never before. Seek the face of God and not His hands. In other words, desire His presence more than anything else and watch how the world around you will change for the better. Take time to keep a clean conduit between you and God. Confess that sin immediately and keep a clean line of communication with the Father. Be full of the Holy Spirit, and obey every instruction of the Lord even when it doesn't make sense.

I want to close out the book by discussing encouragement and godly accountability. This is a huge piece often left out regarding growing your relationship with Jesus Christ. Let's see what God's Word tells us about the importance of having godly influences to keep us strong and on point.

Proverbs 27:17 says, "As iron sharpens iron, so one man sharpens another."

Ecclesiastes 4:9-10: "Two are better than one, because they have a good return for their work: If one falls down, his friend can help him up. But pity the man who falls and has no one to help him up!"

We all need help and accountability. We need each other. There is only so much we can do on our own. I don't know about you, but I need encouragement. There is a limit to what discipline and passion can accomplish. We all face discouragement and challenging times in this life. Being a Christian and living a life of faith is like being in a boxing ring with a powerful opponent. It is a battle. If you are in Christ, your opponent is Satan himself.

John 10:10: "The thief comes to kill, steal, and destroy."

He never gives up, and he doesn't fight fairly at all. We are fighting a spiritual war. You may have taken a few good licks from Satan, and he may have dazed you well, but you must keep fighting. There will be times when you feel like you are just hanging on to get to the bell. My question is this: who is in your corner? Who is your coach? Where is the motivation coming from in your corner? Think about it this way: a professional fighter doesn't do it alone. He surrounds himself with people who can make him better. A fighter surrounds himself with people who have experience and know what is going on. He embraces people who have been there and done that. That boxer needs people around him who know his weaknesses but, more importantly, learn how to make him stronger. Yes, we need people who will push us and people who will be brutally honest with us. We need people around us who will care for us and motivate us to keep on fighting.

Who is in your corner? Who has been there and done that? Who is that person that motivates you? Who is there to encourage and support you? I love to get people thinking by asking questions. I love to see people working things through in their minds and processing how that would look in their lives. I want to ask you four simple questions that have to do with accountability.

1. **Why should you be accountable to someone? It's scriptural! It is encouraged and supported in God's Word.**

Ephesians 5:21: "Summit to one another out of reverence for Christ."

Galatians 6:2: "Carry each other's burdens, and this way you will fulfill the law of Christ."

2 Timothy 2:22: "Flee the evil desires of youth, and pursue righteousness, faith, love, and peace, along with people who call on the Lord out of a pure heart."

Accountability protects you from Satan and helps you build a pure life. As believers in Christ, we are to submit to one another and help to carry each other's burdens of life.

Romans 14:12: "So, then, each of us will give an account of himself in God."

Because I will have to give an account of my entire life to God, I must use every means possible to live a godly life. Accountability works. Our flesh is weak. How often have we started with good intentions and fallen flat on our faces over time? If we go on this journey alone, we will have only ourselves to answer to. But we double our accountability if we tell someone else what we are committing to. I have been trying to write this book for several years. I wanted to do this, but I kept it all to myself. As time passed, I got busy doing other things and lost focus. I never got around to it. Over the last year or two, I told my family and a few friends what I wanted to do. Then, I shared it with my Church family. Now, it is out there, and I have some accountability. And I now have people who are asking how my writing is going. So, I have had to up my game. I had to set aside extra time to see this thing through and dig deeper into my thoughts. Again, accountability works.

This leads to my second question, which has to do with accountability:

2. **Why do you refuse to have an accountability partner if accountability works? The number one reason you do not want someone to hold you accountable is because of selfish pride.**

Proverbs 16:18-19 says, "Pride goes before destruction, a haughty spirit before a fall. Better to be lowly in spirit and among the oppressed than to share plunder with the proud."

Sometimes, We are too proud to let down our guard or remove our spiritual masks. We need to drop the pretense and be willing to share the real me. The second reason we shy away from getting an accountability partner is we lack commitment. We fear what it may cost us. We begin to wonder what we will have to give up going all in with Christ. The third reason we don't want someone in our corner is fear. Many of us are afraid that someone will get to know the real me. They would find out all my weaknesses and issues and then would never look at me the same again. The fourth reason we never took the time to get some accountability is we are just flat lazy. Sometimes in our lives, we don't care and don't want anybody in our faces. Our want to has got up and left the building.

3. What type of person should be your Corner Man?

Proverbs 13:20: "He who walks with the wise grows wise, but a companion of fools suffers harm."

Having someone in your corner who has been where you are would be best. Someone who has been through life's fires and passed the tests. Someone mature in their faith and grounded in the Word of God. It would be best to have someone who doesn't mind calling you out and is willing to ask you difficult questions. But most of all, you need someone who will love you through thick and thin. I ask you again, who is in your corner?

4. What needs to happen with your accountability partner?

First, get to know each other and ask questions about life and their faith. Then, look at your life and see where you are, but also talk about where you want to go. Establish some goals, both short-term and long-term goals. Look at what James 5:16 says:

> *"Therefore, confess your sins to each other and pray for each other so that you may be healed. The prayer of a righteous man is powerful and effective."*

Yes, you need to pray with each other and pray for one other. It would be best if you were willing to be open and honest with each other. Finally, accountability partners must encourage and challenge one another in our faith.

I urge you to get involved in a Bible-believing local body of believers. We all need to sit under the teachings of God's Holy Word and be engaged in some form of a small group. We all need encouragement and support to grow in a way that pleases God. It is good to do life together because God didn't design us to do it alone. Also, begin to pray for that person who could be that accountability partner for you. Then, open your spiritual eyes and ears to what God has for you.

Man up! It is time to step up and go all in with Christ Jesus. We have a mission to complete and a purpose to fulfill. Let no one deter you or distract you. Keep your eyes centered on the Savior of the world, and don't mind the grind. Become a student of His Word and a mighty prayer warrior. Dream big, but pray bigger. To God be the glory forever and ever.

MORE BOOKS BY DENNIS TAYLOR

1. **Fuel For Today:** A 6-Month Devotional Guide For Spiritual Growth And Encouragement
2. **The Total Package:** The Balanced Life
3. **Fuel For Today Volume 2:** A 3-Month Devotional Guide For Spiritual Growth And Encouragement.
4. **Surrendered:** From Stressed To Blessed; Your Best Life In Jesus' Easy Yoke
5. **He Fills My Cup:** A 90-Day Devotional To Refresh And Restore Your Soul; Drink From The Fountain.
6. **Say It Again:** For The Ones On The Front Row
7. **Temptation In Seven Stages**
8. **Sit Down At His Table:** A 6-Month Devotional Guide For Spiritual Growth And Encouragement

ABOUT THE AUTHOR

I started in Student Ministry when I was twenty years old, and it has been my calling for nearly thirty years. My heart was for students to come to know Christ and to grow in their relationship with Him. I love to see God's light bulb fill their eyes and hearts, and I loved sharing the Gospel of Jesus with students whom everybody else said were a lost cause. My passion was to teach them about a relationship with the Lord and give them a real-life example of what it looked like to be walked out in everyday life. My time alone with God has always been my rock, fortress, and high tower. Spending time praying each morning, reading God's Word, and listening to His voice has changed my life forever. I love sharing with young believers who dare to dive deep into the river of God's love. Investing in other people's lives is so rewarding, watching them go from the shallow end of faith and dive into the deep water of a love relationship with Jesus.

I had the privilege of pastoring two Churches, a great blessing to my family and me. First, the Lord led us to plant a Church in Leesburg, Georgia. It was a time of growth and a time of great joy. I loved preaching God's Word weekly and encouraging and loving families. We started with twelve people in our home one Sunday morning; a short time later, God opened the door to purchase a building on a couple of acres in Lee County. That Church is still going strong and is known as Forrester Community Church. I also had the privilege of pastoring Salem Baptist Church in Worth County, Georgia. Salem is a small country Church with a huge heart for God and its community. I was there briefly, but they have a special place in my heart.

Today, I serve as the Pastor of Sports and Recreation at Park Avenue in Titusville, Florida. Peter Lord was the founding pastor of Park Avenue Baptist Church. He was also the author of several well-known books such as Hearing God, Soul Care, 959 Plan, and many more. In addition, he was one of the greatest communicators of God's Word I have ever heard. As the Senior High Student Pastor, I was honored to be discipled by this great man of God in 2004. My role today at Park Avenue is to use sports and recreation to reach out to the community around us. As we develop relationships through sports, God opens the door to share our Jesus with them and their families. My hope, joy, and calling are to lead as many people as possible into a saving relationship with Jesus. Then, please encourage them to take those next steps to grow and mature in their faith.

In 2022, I wrote two devotional books, Fuel for Today Volumes One and Two. I also penned the book The Total Package, which deals with living a balanced life in Christ. My last two chapter books were Say It Again and Surrendered, and my previous devotional is He Fills My Cup and Sit Down At His Table. I married Laura, my high school sweetheart, and we have been happily married for 37 years. The Lord has blessed us with two grown kids; Carsen serves in the Children's ministry at Passion City Church in Atlanta, Georgia. Mackenzie just got married and is currently working in Augusta, Georgia.